TO WILL
ONE
THING

TO WILL ONE THING

Jeremy D. B. Walker

Reflections on Kierkegaard's 'Purity of Heart'

McGILL—QUEEN'S UNIVERSITY PRESS
MONTREAL AND LONDON 1972

© McGill–Queen's University Press 1972

International Standard Book Number: 0–7735–0084–7

Library of Congress Catalog Number: 72–81506

Legal Deposit 3rd quarter 1972

Designed by Mary Cserepy

Printed and bound in Canada by
T. H. Best Printing Company Limited

contents

preface

I would like to acknowledge the help I have received from my colleagues and students. Alistair McKinnon read through the whole work at an early stage, and both Bruce Garside and Seymour Glouberman read parts of it. Students at McGill University and at the University of Minnesota helped to correct and clarify my ideas. However, to me alone must all confusions and eccentricities of this work be imputed.

Chapter one of this book has been previously published in *Kierkegaardiana*, volume 8 (1971), and I thank its editor for permission to republish it here. Chapter seven has been published in *Inquiry*, volume 12 (1969), and I thank its editor also.

For this study the following editions of Kierkegaard's works have been used:

Purity of Heart Is to Will One Thing. Translated and with an introduction by Douglas Steere. New York: Harper & Row, first edition, 1956. All page references are to the Harper Torchbooks edition of this translation.

Concluding Unscientific Postscript. Translated by David F. Swenson. Completed and with an introduction and notes by Walter Lowrie. Princeton: Princeton University Press, 1941.

Either/Or. Translated by David F. Swenson and Lillian Marvin Swenson. With foreword and revisions by Howard A. Johnson. New York: Anchor Books, 1959.

The Journals of Kierkegaard. Edited and translated by Alexander Dru. New York: Fontana, 1958.

On Authority and Revelation. Translated and with an introduction and notes by Walter Lowrie. New York: Harper & Row, 1966.

Works of Love. Translated by Howard Hong and Edna Hong. New York: Harper & Row, 1964.

introduction

have tried in these studies to articulate certain philosophical themes which I believe are implicit in Kierkegaard's *Purity of Heart Is to Will One Thing*. Now *Purity of Heart* is not itself a philosophical work, but rather a 'spiritual preparation for the office of confession'. Moreover, we must not forget its dedication: to 'that individual'. Such a work is obviously far removed from anything like philosophy as this is nowadays understood, an enterprise allegedly characterized by its objectivity, its generality, and its public nature. I have for this reason tried to avoid the error of treating *Purity of Heart* as if it were a philosophical treatise.

But, for all that, it appears to me to be a work in which certain large themes properly described as philosophical may be discerned. By 'philosophical' I mean two related things. First, Kierkegaard's own mind was a profoundly analytical and reflective mind, so that he could not help casting all his thoughts into a philosophical mould, and treating them in a philosophical manner. Second, the very description that he gives of *Purity of Heart* implies that it is designed to inspire in its reader a kind of thoughtful reflection. Admittedly Kierkegaard is pointing towards reflection about oneself, the kind of reflection that is supposed to lead to self-awareness, and in particular to the enlightenment of the conscience. But this intention is not, after all, very dissimilar to the intention in the Socratic Dialogues of Plato. In this tradition 'philosophy' designates a reflective activity which is essentially connected with self-knowledge, and therefore indissoluble from choice and action. I am claiming that we may properly read *Purity of Heart* as a philosophical work of this tradition, which is not to deny that, in its character as a Christian work, it is also intended to go beyond the merely Socratic.

Now when a reader who happens to be a professional philosopher approaches *Purity of Heart*, it would be strange if his individual inclinations and capacities did not enter into his reading of it. It is just here, I hope, that my attempt to read the philosophical elements out of *Purity of Heart* has been most true to its dedication. For I, that individual whose reading of *Purity of Heart* is presented in these studies, am a philosopher, and what would be less honest than to try to disguise this fact in my interpretation?

Nonetheless, I have tried to read and understand *Purity of Heart* as its author meant it to be read and understood. That is to say, I have tried to read it as a work, in the Socratic tradition, part of whose innermost function is to aid its individual reader to clarify his self-reflections. To this, all other considerations, including detailed questions of philosophical analysis and scholarship, have been held subordinate, by which I do not, of course, mean irrelevant or unimportant.

My book is, however, not a commentary upon *Purity of Heart*, or not a commentary in any ordinary sense of that word. I have not discussed much that is in that work, for example its final sections, entitled 'What Then Must I Do?'. Nor does the order of my discussion follow the order of Kierkegaard's presentation. Nor have I tried to give a series of explanatory elucidations of the actual text, even in respect of those parts of it upon which I have reflected. My reflections, then, are not an attempt to translate Kierkegaard's statements into some other idiom, for instance the idiom of contemporary analytical philosophy.

Nor, again, have I tried to write a scholarly analysis of *Purity of Heart*. I do not, for example, attempt here seriously to trace historical influences and resemblances between the thought of Kierkegaard and, say, Kant, or Saint Augustine. Nor do I attempt to trace the connections between *Purity of Heart* and Kierkegaard's other works. (A partial exception to this is the final chapter of my book.) The reason for these omissions is not that I believe there would be no good in the attempt at a broad comparative discussion of Kierkegaard's many ethical writings. On the contrary, such an attempt would be of the greatest value, and I intend sometime in the future to try to write a descriptive treatise on Kierkegaard's ethics. The present work, however, is not that, and, as I hope I have made clear, not a work of that type at all. It is much rather an 'existential' confrontation with just one of Kierkegaard's major works, one of that late group all of which are designed to provoke self-reflection, and the only one of this group which is explicitly devoted to the idea of commitment.

Since *Purity of Heart* is one of Kierkegaard's acknowledged works, I have not felt it necessary to express my opinions here on the difficult problem of the views found in the pseudonymous works, and their relations to Kierkegaard's own acknowledged views. This will be a task for the descriptive treatise I mentioned. However, it seems to me that each pseudonymous work requires careful and intense study on its own, and that this must encompass its rhetoric as well as its philosophy. Generalizations about the views of the pseudonyms can only follow such detailed study, not precede it.

Similarly, in these studies I have referred at several points to the Kantian ethics, or to analytical distinctions taken as characteristic of a Kantian ethics. It would not be going too far to say that I have superimposed these 'Kantian' concepts on Kierkegaard's *Purity of Heart*, given a Kantian reading of this work. Such a judgement is fair, provided in turn the notion of a Kantian type of ethics be itself given a provisional and ill-defined interpretation. I have not thought it possible in a work of this kind to go into the profound problems of Kant scholarship and interpretation. I have taken it for granted that there is a readily recognizable Kantian tradition in moral philosophy, and have attempted in these studies, *inter alia*, to make a case for placing *Purity of Heart* partly within this tradition.

What I have tried to do here is to *re-think* the thought-path traced out by Kierkegaard in *Purity of Heart*. I have called this book *To Will One Thing: Reflections on Kierkegaard's 'Purity of Heart.'* I could also have described it as a series of 'reflections of' Kierkegaard's own book — reflections from one mind (and time) into another. That by itself would be over-simple. It applies to the first four chapters of this book, but not so well to the remainder. Chapters five and six are explicitly philosophical in content, in a way in which their predecessors are not. My book moves from a series of philosophical reflections (broad sense) on the central moral argument of *Purity of Heart*, to a philosophical study (narrow sense) of the implicit moral philosophy behind Kierkegaard's argument. The moral argument is not independent of this moral philosophy: on the other hand, the moral philosophy gets its existential import from the actual moral argument. So all moral reflection, carried beyond a certain depth, necessarily becomes philosophical reflection on the nature of morality: conversely, moral philosophizing has no existential relevance, unless it arises out of some moral 'problematic', or is directed towards its clarification and resolution — in action.

One comment on this work suggested that, although I began in philosophy, I ended in theology. I am prepared to accept this suggestion, on condition that I be allowed to add that neither term appears to me to denote anything very distinct. It is true that I have mentioned some ancient theological problems in chapter six, in particular the problems involved in the ideas of human freedom and divine grace. Nor would I deny that Kierkegaard himself was profoundly versed in theology, and that for this reason it is highly probable that the 'ethical' arguments of *Purity of Heart* are susceptible of a parallel 'theological' development. But, for all that, *Purity of Heart* is not a treatise in theology. If it holds a lesson in this regard for its reader, it may be that an existential reflection of the kind it demands cannot but lead the individual reflecter into a realm of ideas long fought over by theologians. In this sense, if Kierkegaard is right, moral reflection drives us all into theology: perhaps in this sense only. For these reasons, added to my awareness of my own incompetence in theology, I have thought it worthwhile to allude to some of these implicit theological problems, but to do no more than allude to their possible presence.

The central philosophical theme of *Purity of Heart* is the idea of *commitment*. Commitment has become an important subject of contemporary ethical discussion, primarily in relation to the ethics of existentialism, but in an interesting secondary sense in relation to certain branches of 'linguistic' or analytical ethics, for example, the work of R. M. Hare. It is no accident that there are notable similarities between the ethics of Hare and Sartre. For both men's ethical views have been very strongly influenced by Kant, especially by his views concerning the logical functions of reason in relation to moral decision. An ethics of commitment is an essentially Kantian ethics.

The concept of commitment is also absolutely fundamental to Kierkegaard's whole thought, both in its earliest appearances (for example, *Fear and Trembling*), and in its latest (for example, *The Attack upon Christendom*). Kierkegaard treats this concept very variously in his writings: now under one aspect (the concept of passion, the concept of love, the concept of faith), now under another: now in respect of one implication (the concept of suffering, the concept of the individual, the concept of the self and its modes of despair), now in respect of another. Only in *Purity of Heart* does he place the concept of commitment itself openly in the centre of his discussion. And only in this work does he deliberately give to his discussion an ethical import, as contrasted with a Christian one. *Fear and Trembling*, for example, is devoted to similar problems, but these are *explicitly* related to the question of the individual's relation to God. It is true that *Purity of Heart* is also explicitly a religious work, in some sense. Its title page and its opening and closing reflections make that indisputable. However the bulk of the book is cast quite unmistakably in terms specific to an ethics that is not Christian. For instance, God is referred to throughout by means of the Platonising term 'The Good'. This cannot be either accidental or insignificant, in a writer as careful and rhetorically skilful as Kierkegaard. Moreover, in his *Journals* Kierkegaard characterizes *Purity of Heart* as an *aesthetic* work: he writes, 'The plan is essentially *ethico-ironic*' (my italics). But what is the significance of the method used in *Purity of Heart*? What does Kierkegaard intend his reader to understand by its specific rhetoric, and what does he wish him to infer from this?

About the first part of the answer to these questions, there can be little serious doubt. Kierkegaard is putting forward a pair of claims about commitment. First, he argues that *genuine* commitment must be *total* commitment, in a sense he explains. To argue this is to argue that partial commitment cannot be genuine commitment. Second, he argues that total commitment is conceivable only as commitment to 'The Good' which, as I have said, is used as a term referring to God, but whose actual content is specifically and merely ethical. I have tried in my book to show that Kierkegaard is arguing, on the purely ethical level, that ethics must begin with an acknowledgement of what Kant called the autonomy of the will, but need not and cannot end either with Kant's own merely formal principle (the categorical imperative), or with a total absence of objective moral principles (Hare and Sartre). Kierkegaard shows, if he is successful, that fully understanding the idea of the will's autonomy is coming to understand that the will is only really autonomous when its object is 'The Good'. If this is indeed the correct interpretation of the ethical intentions of *Purity of Heart*, then, whether or not Kierkegaard succeeds in his argument, his book must be of the first importance to ethics; not only to a study of Kantian ethics, but also to a study of those contemporary ethical theories in which the same problems crop up. Still more important, of course, will be its bearing upon each individual's own concrete moral reflections and decisions.

The second part of the answer to the question of the significance of the mode of argument used in *Purity of Heart* must be more open to doubt. I believe the answer is something like the following. Suppose someone's ethical reflections begin with an attempt to understand the idea of commitment. If Kierkegaard is right, he will sooner or later come to realize that while commitment is inescapable, it is possible only if its object is 'The Good'. This, then, will be the unavoidable conclusion of a reflection that begins in the purely ethical sphere. But it now becomes clear that this reflection has not remained entirely within the ethical sphere, regarded as something distinct from the religious. (In the pseudonymous theory of the 'Stages', it is only Christianity from which the ethical is sharply distinct; the various sub-Christian religiosities are not sharply distinct from the ethical, as is implied by the second part of *Either/Or*.) For it has become clear that the idea of 'The Good' can be identified only with the idea of the God of Christianity. Kierkegaard's argument is thus as much a refutation of a non-Christian Platonistic ethics as it is a refutation of a purely Kantian, or existentialist, ethics. The inner logic of ethical reflection, therefore, suffices to transform it into a mode of Christian reflection — a mode of the Christian consciousness. (Here we may perhaps detect a hint of the theory of the Stages.) This, then, is a sketch of what I believe the answer to be. Again, if I am right, Kierkegaard's work must have momentous consequences for all ethics, as well as for the reflections of the individual.

If my reading of *Purity of Heart* is close to the truth, then some familiar conceptions of 'Kierkegaard's ethics' stand in need of severe and careful revision. To illustrate this claim, I shall discuss one such conception, put forward in the work of an acknowledged expert on Kierkegaard, Professor James Collins.

Professor Collins devotes chapter three of his useful treatise, *The Mind of Kierkegaard*, to an examination of Kierkegaard's ideas concerning 'The Ethical View and Its Limits'. In this chapter, which is mainly a discussion of *Either/Or* and *Stages on Life's Way* together with *Fear and Trembling*, Professor Collins is concerned chiefly to analyse Kierkegaard's view of the ethical, regarded as the second of the three familiar Stages, or world-views, flanked by the aesthetic on one hand and the religious on the other. He therefore discusses three points: the ethical 'revaluation' of the aesthetic world-view; the nature of ethical choice and the 'final end'; and the religious transcendence of the ethical world-view. He begins by claiming that 'ethics as a formal philosophical standpoint and prevalent attitude meant for him Kantian ethics' (Chicago: Gateway Editions, 1965, p. 68). Although this is to underestimate the influence of Hegel's concept of *Sittlichkeit* on Kierkegaard, I am so far in agreement with Professor Collins. He continues, however, as follows: 'Because he saw the danger to religion in an autonomous conception of morality and yet was unacquainted with any philosophical treatment which escapes this pitfall, Kierkegaard did not reach any rigorously philosophical solution of the problems of moral life' (p. 68). But, according to my reading of it, *Purity of Heart* contains just that 'philosophical treatment', and that 'rigorously philosophical solution', whose existence Professor Collins denies. Further, far from seeing a danger to religion in the morality of autonomism, I have tried to show that Kierkegaard in fact sees this morality as requiring Christianity as its logical and existential coping stone, while also, I believe, seeing true religion as necessarily founded upon autonomous morality.

Professor Collins argues that the religious transcendence of ethics is implicitly discussed in *Fear and Trembling*. He is careful to point out that the Abraham story is not here told by Kierkegaard, but is put into the mouth of the pseudonymous Johannes de Silentio. He remarks, correctly, that this should alert us to place 'certain qualifications' on the theory. However he appears to accept it in its essentials as Kierkegaard's own view. What, then, is involved in the famous 'teleological suspension of the ethical'? Professor Collins argues that the important contrast to which Kierkegaard is pointing is between the ethical *universal* and the *individual* human subject. Ethical universalism cannot account for, and stands in contradiction with, the possibility that an existing individual may be brought into immediate relation to God. Thus 'religious duties' following from such a relation cannot but appear, from the ethical viewpoint, as contraventions of moral duty. Here religion has the higher claim upon the individual, so that the ethical must temporarily be 'suspended' or 'transcended'.

I have argued in this book that in *Purity of Heart* Kierkegaard shows that the kind of commitment required within the Kantian ethical world-view cannot contradict, but actually requires, the kind of commitment characteristic of Christianity, that is, a commitment towards God. If so, the account of the 'teleological suspension' that is given by Johannes de Silentio, and accepted by Professor Collins, directly conflicts with Kierkegaard's own conception of the relation between ethics and religion. I believe the source of Professor Collins' error is his assumption that Johannes can be taken as essentially expressing Kierkegaard's own views. On the contrary, we now have to suppose, if I am right, that he is expressing a view of ethics and religion that is in some respects fundamentally mistaken from Kierkegaard's own viewpoint. The fundamental mistake is the mislocation of the central logical feature of ethics. Johannes assumes, and Professor Collins follows him, that the ethical is centrally characterized by its *universalism*, in contrast to the *individualism* central to the aesthetic world-view. Certainly universalism is an important feature of the Kantian (and Hegelian) ethics. Nevertheless it seems to me to be a secondary feature, at any rate for Kant. The primary and central feature is surely rather *autonomism*: after all, Kant calls the will's autonomy 'the supreme principle of morality', and his universalism is a kind of deduction from his supreme principle. (It is precisely here that Johannes, and Judge William in *Either/Or*, represent Hegel far more accurately than Kant: both submerge the principle of the will's autonomy in the principle of the universality of the ethical demand.) Thus it comes to appear to Johannes that ethics is essentially opposed to the *individualism* of the aesthetic, and that the higher *individualism* of Christianity must also be essentially opposed to the principle of ethics. In truth, I believe Kierkegaard himself saw these contrasts quite differently. For him the essential contrast was that ethics puts the individual *will* at its centre, whereas the aesthetic viewpoint, having no coherent concept of the will, circles around the idea of the individual's feelings and moods (his passivity). (A Fichteanism in Kierkegaard.) In a sense, therefore, the contrast is that the aesthetic contains no coherent conception of the individual as *subject*, whereas the ethical is constructed around just this concept. Further, it seems to me that Kierkegaard, while accepting Kant's basic autonomism, actually rejects the rationalistic universalism which Kant sees as implied, and which for a poor Kantian such as Johannes has swallowed up and hidden from his eyes the prior Kantian doctrine of autonomy. Not only is the true Kierkegaardian contrast between ethics and aesthetics thus misrepresented in *Fear and Trembling* (and *Either/Or*); so, more importantly, is the relation between ethics and religion. For if Johannes is mistaken in claiming that the ethical is essentially universal, whereas the religious centres upon the idea of the individual's immediate relation to God, it follows that there is no longer any necessity for a 'teleological suspension' of ethics in the face of the religious demand. Indeed, in my view, the ethical concept of the individual as an autonomous willing subject, far from conflicting with any essential presupposition of Christianity, is for Kierkegaard precisely one of Christianity's essential presuppositions. *Purity of Heart* may be read as Kierkegaard's own unfolding of this concept, and his demonstration that this implies not, as Kant thought, a merely formal universal principle of reason, but the teleology of an objective and absolute good, which can be identified only with the incarnate God of Christianity. (I believe that a parallel metaphysical deduction is latent within *Sickness Unto Death*.) It follows that it is also wrong to suppose that Kierkegaard's conception of ethics can be adequately described by merely considering the Kierkegaardian treatments of the ethical as one among three Stages. In fact, I believe that the very conception of ethics as an intermediate stage must belong not to Kierkegaard himself — for whom this conception is mistaken — but only to the pseudonymous characters who express this view.

The doctrine of the teleological suspension of the ethical raises, in a specific form, the problem of the relation between reason and faith in Kierkegaard's thought. It is most commonly held that Kierkegaard himself was an 'irrationalist' or a 'fideist', whatever precisely such terms mean. On the other hand some, notably Father Cornelio Fabro, have argued that for Kierkegaard himself the reason/faith opposition is not 'essential', but merely 'existential'. (See his masterly essay 'Faith and Reason in Kierkegaard's Dialectic', translated and published in *A Kierkegaard Critique*, edited by Howard Johnson and Niels Thulstrup [New York: Harper & Row, 1962]). However it remains true that Kierkegaard's resolution of the problem is a world away from the rationalisms of Kant and Hegel. Now my book does not touch upon this problem, even indirectly. Nevertheless, there is an interesting indirect relation between the problem of reason and faith, and the actual problems which I have tried to analyse.

The first point is that the reason/faith distinction cannot, for Kierkegaard, coincide with the ethics/religion distinction (assuming, for the moment, that there is one). Admittedly, some of the pseudonymous works seem to imply such a coincidence, for example, *Fear and Trembling* and, perhaps, *Philosophical Fragments*. However others do not, most notably *Concluding Unscientific Postscript* and Kierkegaard's own acknowledged *Works of Love*. The most obvious reason why the equation fails is that, if the sphere of faith is taken as religion, then the sphere of reason must embrace both the ethical and the aesthetic, at least on the standard view of the relation of ethics and religion in Kierkegaard.

I have argued, however, that this standard view is itself mistaken. It rests upon wrongly ascribing to Kierkegaard himself descriptions of ethics that are uttered by certain pseudonyms. In my book, I have tried to show that for Kierkegaard there can be no coherent ethical viewpoint that does not find itself driven, by its own inner logic, to accepting the idea of God as its coping stone. An ethics that includes the act of faith as its coping stone will for the first time constitute a complete and coherent ethical viewpoint, since it is the first adequate expression of that total commitment which is the presupposition for the possibility of any 'ethics'. An ethics that does not include the act of faith must, for Kierkegaard, remain essentially incomplete and incoherent *as an ethical viewpoint* since, although presupposing the need for a total commitment, it cannot find any adequate object for such a commitment. If so, any presentation of ethics that makes ethics out to be excluded from, or opposed to, religion must be thus far directly contrary to Kierkegaard's own view. Briefly, I hold that for Kierkegaard himself the 'leap' of faith, whatever it is, cannot be a leap out of, or beyond, the sphere of ethics; on the contrary, it is only with and through that leap that the sphere of ethics for the first time becomes complete and coherent as an ethical sphere.

In my book I have not discussed the question of faith and reason. The allusions to the concept of faith in chapter seven are a partial exception to this generalization, but even there the question is by no means asked or answered openly. I have implicitly argued that for Kierkegaard ethics demands and implies faith. Whether or not this means that ethics is in part contrary to, or beyond, reason depends on whether faith is contrary to, or beyond, reason. My own view, for which I have not argued in my book, is that for Kierkegaard himself faith always remained in some respects *essentially* contrary to reason. Thus my own view is that for Kierkegaard even the ethical cannot be comprehended within the limits of (natural) reason. Kierkegaard goes decisively beyond Kant and Hegel at this point. God, far from remaining a mere presupposition for the possibility of ethics, must be the actual object of the ethical will. Therefore the ethical and the religious are, in a sense, one sphere. They are one sphere regarded in two different ways. This sphere is 'the religious', when understood as the sphere of the individual's immediate relation to God. It is 'the ethical', when understood as the sphere of the individual's free engagement of himself in activity. I believe this is a lesson of *Works of Love*.

For Kierkegaard himself, then, the sphere of reason can at most coincide with the aesthetic stage. Now *Purity of Heart* contains a series of implicit contrasts between the ethical and the prudential, or 'reasonable', way of looking at things. It follows, if this latter identification is justified, that Kierkegaard will in such passages be implicitly contrasting the ethical solution to life's problems with their aesthetic 'solution'. However this account cannot be entirely correct or complete, if only because it is doubtful that Kierkegaard thought there could be any coherent and self-contained 'rational' outlook upon life. *Philosophical Fragments*, for example, seems to argue that rationalism eventually meets with unavoidable psychological *and logical* blocks. Chapter three of that work appears to present an argument that there is a 'natural dialectic of reason' which inevitably leads reason to collide with 'the Paradox'. Although an interesting parallel to Kant's argument, what Kierkegaard (or rather Johannes Climacus) says is again not purely Kantian, since this collision is ascribed not to the internal logic of natural reason, but partly to the *passion* of reason, and partly to the independent activity of 'the Paradox'.

It is widely thought that for Kierkegaard the 'transition' from the ethical to the religious stage is chiefly, or solely, *psychological*. On this view, roughly enough, Kierkegaard argues that a purely ethical outlook upon life must break down for psychological reasons. The ethical individual must come to experience a particular kind of despair, and only by making the act of repentance can he possibly rise above his despair, thus entering the sphere of religion. I do not deny the existence of this 'psychological argument' in Kierkegaard. But it seems to me that it must, even on its own terms, be supplemented by considerations of a quite different kind, namely, metaphysical-ontological considerations. For it must presuppose a more or less tacit metaphysics (ontology) of the human self. And is this not made quite clear in *Sickness Unto Death*? However, what I have tried to show in this book goes still further. If my reading of *Purity of Heart* is correct, Kierkegaard provides us with the sketch of a *logical* theory of the transition from the ethical to the religious. The fundamental concept of ethics, that of commitment — a concept accepted equally by Kantians, existentialists, and Kierkegaard himself — is shown to be *logically* coherent only if completed by the act of faith.

It now may be asked what relevance a philosophical discussion of Kierkegaard's concept of commitment can have to someone faced with the problems of living in the later twentieth century. This question is right and proper. The activity of philosophy cannot be supposed to justify itself. For it represents just one possible existential commitment among others, one way of using one's available time and talents.

The first, and broadest, answer must be that, since we cannot escape from the burden of making our own individual lives, it follows that we cannot avoid the need to make one or another fundamental commitment of ourselves. This entails the need of reflection, and in particular reflection upon the possible objects of such fundamental commitment; and behind that, a deeper reflection on the ultimate grounds of any such commitment, the principles by which one commitment is justified over against the alternative possibilities. Here, driven into moral thinking, we are, as I have said, inescapably driven into philosophical thinkin about morality, that is, into moral philosophizing. Thus, although the profession of moral philosopher is just one possible commitment among others, moral philosophy is a necessary element of every possible commitment. There can be no short cuts for any free and rational individual.

The second answer, which brings the question of relevance down to the precise subject at issue, is as follows. All moral thinking has ultimately the form: 'What Then Must I Do?' (Perhaps it has, rather, the primary form: 'What Then Must We Do?'; to this Tolstoyan, and Marxist, formulation I turn briefly below.) The fundamental question is asked concerning particular courses of action and actions. But it must also be asked about the whole course of one's life. And the answer to each particular asking of it must imply, in the background, some answer to the general question. Moral thinking, then, cannot be only concerned with particular decisions and choices, nor even with particular 'projects'. It must be concerned, and this most fundamentally, with the kind of ultimate and general choice or commitment that is expressed in the whole course and direction of an individual's life. Most of our thinking on these matters, of course, is confused and illusory: it is guided by imagination, self-deception, and fear: it falls short of the required virtues of honesty, seriousness, and courage. Few among us succeed in openly facing the terrifying question: is my life on the right course? . . .

These are precisely the questions which Kierkegaard poses, and answers, in *Purity of Heart*. Now his answers may not be found agreeable: they may not be judged correct. But *Purity of Heart* is numbered among the handful of works which have analysed the question to its profoundest depths. In our own time, perhaps only Dietrich Bonhoeffer and Simone Weil can stand beside Kierkegaard. They are among the exemplary figures of our time, and their reflections too should be ours.

Bonhoeffer and Simone Weil were essentially political thinkers. So too, in his peculiar way, was Kierkegaard, although his reflections here necessarily have a distance from our situation which theirs do not have. It is often said that morality and moral commitment must be political in our time. This is true, but it is also a truism. For it is necessarily true of all times, of all situations. It was true of Kierkegaard's own time, the European 1840s. Kierkegaard stood beside another thinker of comparable power and depth, one who exhibited the same intellectual virtues of honesty, seriousness, and courage. That thinker was Karl Marx. Now Marx's answers to these deep questions were extremely different from Kierkegaard's. In some respects their thought was in radical conflict. I say radical, since this conflict lies right at the roots of their thought. For Kierkegaard man is essentially a subjective being. For Marx man is essentially an objective being. Marx does not, of course, mean by this anything like 'objective' in the sense so fiercely attacked by Kierkegaard in *The Present*

Age. On the contrary, Marx is as strongly opposed to this kind of 'objectivity' as Kierkegaard is. Both built their thought upon the belief that man is a being who cannot avoid commitment, and therefore must not try to evade it. They shared, in part, a vision of their world: they both diagnosed it as an 'objective' world, a world intellectually and spiritually dominated by the spirit of objectivity. In reaction against this spirit, they both called their readers to remember that man is fundamentally a being of will or action who, therefore, cannot avoid acting, however much he tries to disguise this from himself.

Our time is schizophrenic. It is split between a passionless objectivity and an unreflective enthusiasm. Our paradigms of objectivity are not those attacked by Kierkegaard and Marx. We are not faced by a 'System' with pretensions to comprehend the totality of world-history and human creativity. Our objectivists are at once more modest and more radical. In abandoning the vision of the ideal unity of the human world, they have also abandoned the ideal of humanity. In opposition to this spirit, we have already begun to see the relevance of the Marxian demand for commitment, stripped of historically accidental features. But even here our Marxism is characteristic of our time, falling apart into two disconnected and contrary ideologies: on the one hand, a Marxism itself infected by objectivism and emptied of its humanism and idealism; on the other, a Marxism so opposed to theorizing as to have become a practically pure ahistorical voluntarism. In Marx's own sight, the revolutionary commitment and the radical theory of man were inseparable. Our subjectivism, however, is not a genuine passion, in Kierkegaard's terms. He would have called our time not a time of revolution, but a time of rebelliousness. (This applies to the West only.) Our subjectivists, too, are simultaneously less consistent and more radical than those of the 1840s, the romantics. They have erected their 'Systems' of subjectivism, but in so doing have emptied human subjectivity of all recognizable human content. Their individualisms acknowledge no basis for the ethical life, the life of community, or the existence of common goals for humanity. Just as we have two Marxes, we have two Kierkegaards. One is the name for a total and unmitigated subjectivity. The other is the subject of a theological and philosophical systematization. Kierkegaard himself foresaw the probability of the latter fate: he did not foresee the possibility of the former, and he would have regarded it as infinitely the more disastrous.

There can be, I believe, no valid 'synthesis' of the Marxian and the Kierkegaardian answers to the fundamental question of commitment. Their radical humanisms are in immediate opposition. Nor can there be, I believe, a third answer, given the exhaustiveness of their opposing humanisms. It is not possible to evade the question. Therefore the basic question for our time, as for all times, can be put: Marx or Kierkegaard?

My book falls into three roughly separable parts. In chapters one to four, I present a series of studies of some of the concepts and arguments most central to Kierkegaard's idea of commitment, in particular the concepts of reward and punishment in morality. In exploring the nature of these concepts, I have tried to explore in a Kierkegaardian way some of the grounds for his rejection of a teleological ethics and, more generally, of any ethics based on a principle of the heteronomy of the will. In chapters five and six I present two closely linked studies of certain logical features of Kierkegaard's own concept of commitment, or 'purity of heart'. It is in these two chapters that I have tried to show how Kierkegaard, in my view, deploys this concept so as to demonstrate the necessity for the truly committed will to be wholly turned towards God. I have, therefore, also had to try to show that this demonstration is not inconsistent with Kierkegaard's original position, but does, on the other hand, succeed in going beyond the bare Kantian position. These two chapters contain the outlines of my central thesis, and it is in the development of the argument I have there constructed that Kierkegaard's unique attempt to 'synthesize' the fundamental insights of Kantian and

Platonistic ethics in a new 'Christian ethics' may be explained. A more detailed examination of this idea, however, I have rightly or wrongly considered a task for another work. The final chapter presents a study of a rather different kind from the others. For all its difference of character, I think that the results of the argument in this chapter are substantially in agreement with the interpretation put forward in the previous ones, and they may illuminate some of the relations between *Purity of Heart* and other Kierkegaardian works and themes.

These studies will be found deficient in many respects. Sometimes the reader will perceive contradictory remarks and conflicting views. Arguments will be discovered which break off before reaching any satisfactory conclusion. I have not always been able to make very clear the relevance of particular matters to the great point at issue. Many conceptual analyses, for example those in chapter two, are obscure, tentative, and imperfect. But it would have been dishonest of me, had I tried to impose a harmonious and coherent appearance on the presentation of my thinking, for any such harmony could have been only false. In much of this thinking I have not yet succeeded in achieving any final and coherent opinions on the profound issues with which Kierkegaard fought. In this respect, also, my book is offered as an existential reflection upon *Purity of Heart*, in that it reflects the authentic difficulties of the intellect experienced by an individual attempting to confront the problems raised in that work.

CHAPTER I   # The idea of reward in morality

o will the Good for the sake of reward is double-mindedness. To will one thing is, therefore, to will the Good without considering the reward' (Kierkegaard, *Purity of Heart*, p. 72).

I am going to try to explain what this remark might mean: some of the many possible things it might mean.

We should bear in mind that all through Kierkegaard is operating with a presumption which influences the logic of his argument. This is the presumption that willing the Good is willing one thing and, conversely, willing one thing is willing the Good. By calling this a presumption, I do not mean that he does not argue for it. He argues for it, and his arguments follow the lines of tradition. But I shall not be examining these arguments until chapter five and six.

Consider the idea of a man's willing the Good—whatever exactly this means—for the sake of the reward. I do not mean necessarily for the sake of something particular that he has set his heart on. I mean only that he believes that for willing the Good there is somewhere laid up something that will reward him sometime—he knows neither where, nor when, nor what.

Now it is plain that in this man's thinking there are two factors at work: the idea of the Good that is the object of his will, and the idea of the reward. The two are distinct. The reward that is to come to him as a reward for willing the Good cannot be identical with the Good that he wills, whatever this may be. It looks at once as if such a man cannot really be described as 'willing one thing,' for he wills the Good, but has also set his heart on the reward. It would follow on Kierkegaard's view that he cannot really be described as 'willing the Good' at all. What passes in such a man for willing the Good must, then, be a spurious and illusory kind of willing the Good. Either the willing, or its object, must be spurious and illusory.

The two factors in this man's thinking are naturally conceived as related in a particular way. The idea of the reward is the operative factor in his will; we might call the reward the 'end', the goal, of the willing and of whatever activity this involves. Then the willing can be no more than the means he adopts to gain this end, and his idea of the Good will simply be his idea of what has to be willed in order to gain the reward. So it is quite possible that for him what he sees as the Good may appear as something which he would not will were it not for the reward to come.

Now we have to make a distinction. For how is willing the Good thought to be related to gaining the reward?

If it is thought that there is just a 'contingent', that is, a causal or quasi-mechanical connection between willing the Good and gaining the reward, then it must also appear that willing the Good may be only one possible way of gaining the reward. And then it must appear at least possible that there is a better way of gaining the reward. 'Better' is ambiguous. For example, our man may think it possible that there is a way of gaining the reward which involves less time, less effort, or less suffering. If he has a definite idea of the reward, especially if he conceives the reward in terms of the natural goods of this world, this is even more likely. For successful deceit seems a better and safer way of getting, say, money or fame than honesty does.

On the other hand, if he believes that genuinely willing the Good must be the best way, perhaps the only possible way, of gaining the reward, then clearly he is under the influence of an a priori presumption. He is presuming some kind of noncontingent, 'necessary' relation between willing the Good and gaining the reward. If, like Kierkegaard, he claims that the reward is *certain*, then obviously he is not thinking in terms of what actually does or might happen.

One way in which he may see a necessary connection between willing the Good and gaining the reward is this: he sees a *conceptual* connection, perhaps because he understands willing the Good as 'doing what will gain the reward' — a kind of utilitarian 'getting what a man will get for willing the Good'. Roughly, he defines the reward in terms of the Good. This way of thinking is clearly more likely to characterize the man who has no definite idea of the kind of reward to be expected, who simply believes that somewhere there is something laid up for him to receive at some time, he knows not when nor where.

Now we have to consider what is involved in the idea of a 'reward *for* willing the Good', and in general the idea of a 'reward'.

Obviously not every good, or desired, thing that comes to me as a result of what I do or say counts as a reward for my deeds or words. And obviously not everything that I am given as a reward need be for me good or desirable, although it must have seemed so to the givers. You would not be 'rewarding' somebody unless you gave him something you believed he would appreciate.

In the most common sort of case, there is no necessary relation between my doing whatever I do and my getting whatever counts as the reward for doing it. For the reward is *given* for doing this, and the decision whether or not to give a reward, and, if so, what to make it, is obviously up to the people who give it. We might call this sort of relationship 'purely conventional'.

But we also speak of 'rewards' and 'being rewarded' in cases where there is no relationship of that sort. For I might be rewarded for what seemed a tedious study of counterpoint by a sudden understanding and appreciation of a whole area of music which had previously been nothing to me. This is a reward, but not a prize, for the study of counterpoint! This is an interesting case, for it seems very relevant to the case of the reward for willing the Good that I am studying. A number of its special features will bring out this relevance.

Unlike the common sort of case, no human agency is involved · in my gaining the reward I do gain: probably no agency at all. We may be tempted to say that it just depends on the operation of some complex and no doubt undiscovered laws of psychology.

Again, there does not seem to be a purely external and con- ·

tingent, still less a purely conventional, relation between the nature of my activity and the nature of the reward. It is much more like the relation between running fast and getting tired than the relation between running fast (winning the race) and getting a silver cup.

And most important of all, there is something about my reward which I could not have foreseen or understood. Of course, I may have known other people who studied counterpoint and, as a result, came to appreciate whole areas of music which had previously meant nothing to them. So in a sense I might well have foreseen and understood the possibility of the same sort of thing happening to me. And I might easily have hoped for this. But what I could not have foreseen is what it was going to be like to come to appreciate this meaningless region of experience.

My being thus rewarded does not depend on my having hoped for this reward. It does not depend on my having studied counterpoint *for the sake of* coming to appreciate, say, sixteenth-century music. I may be suddenly and quite unexpectedly rewarded by finding a good where maybe I have never even expected to find a good. But obviously my having hoped to be rewarded in this way does not in the least prejudice the outcome: no more than would hoping to win a race and the silver cup prejudice the getting the cup. Silver cups are not given only on condition that the winners have been running for the sake of the race but *not* the silver cup!

Willing the Good, whatever exactly this means, may be accompanied or followed by the winning of good or desired things. Honesty is sometimes rewarded. It might be rewarded either by some human agency (the man whose wallet I have returned decides to give me five dollars), or in the kind of way exemplified above. Respect, honour, and perhaps even fame and power, can be 'rewards' for virtue. Aristeides was rewarded for his justice by becoming known as Aristeides the Just.

Moralists and moral philsophers have always tried to minimize the value of suchlike 'rewards' for virtue — for willing the Good.

But their reasons have not always been clear. One obvious consideration is this. Money, fame, and even respect can all too easily go to the man who does not really deserve them — though this description is already somewhat odd. Apparent virtue can be rewarded, in the world's sense of 'reward', just as easily as can genuine virtue, and perhaps more easily.

Another, less obvious consideration is this. What the virtuous or the talented man gets 'as a reward' for his virtue or talent, that is, the money or the fame or the respect, may be only on the surface a reward for his virtue or talent: only an 'apparent reward'. What does this mean?

What is at issue here is a strange conception. It is the idea that the *true reward* for any kind of activity must be *homogeneous* with that activity in a particular sense, that any good which is not homogeneous with the activity can be no more than an 'apparent reward' for it.

The idea of homogeneity is partly explained by the idea of an internal relation. Running fast and winning races, studying counterpoint and coming to appreciate sixteenth-century music, are 'homogeneous'; there is 'homogeneity' between the activity and its reward. Running fast and winning silver cups, studying counterpoint and becoming famed as a conductor, are not homogeneous. The idea in connection with the subject of this chapter is that for willing the Good, too, there can be both a 'true' and 'apparent' reward: that a mark of the true reward will be its homogeneity with willing the Good, as a mark of the merely apparent reward will be its heterogeneity.

This idea, I have said, is explained in part by the idea of an internal, noncontingent, nonconventional relationship between an activity and the good acquired as the outcome of this activity. But it is also, I think, partly explained, or at least illuminated, by considering the traditional distinction between 'instrumental' and 'intrinsic' goods.

I have said that one man might run for the sake of the pickings to be got out of running, another simply in order to win.

Now you might run for neither of these reasons, but simply for the sheer enjoyment of running. Again, one man might study counterpoint because he liked it, another only because he hoped to acquire fame or wealth thereby. And I suppose (like the second case above) you might study counterpoint with the idea of becoming the best contrapuntist alive!

The man who runs for the sheer enjoyment of running, and the man who studies counterpoint because he likes it, are commonly said to be doing what they do 'for its own sake'. And this is commonly contrasted with doing it 'in order to get something out of it'. Or, in the latter case, the activity is simply the means to some further and distinct end; in the former case the activity is the end in itself. For one the activity is a good only 'instrumentally', that is, as a way of getting something acknowledged as good in itself: for the other the activity is a good 'intrinsically'.

I think, though I am unable to argue here, that the idea of instrumentality used in this distinction is the idea of an external and contingent relation. If I am right in this conjecture, it follows that any relation conceived as internal and noncontingent will also be conceived as 'noninstrumental'. It will not be conceived in terms of means and end. Roughly, the means and the end must be conceived as things, or events, related to each other only externally and contingently.

Asked why you study counterpoint, you may answer, 'Oh, I just like it', or 'Because I want to become the most famous conductor in the world'. There are other answers too. Roughly, we may say: the first sort of answer expresses your appreciation of studying counterpoint as an intrinsic good, the second expresses your belief that it is an instrumental good, and most likely describes the kind of end—intrinsic good—which makes it, for you, instrumentally good.

Becoming the most famous conductor in the world as a result of studying counterpoint is an obvious example of getting a heterogeneous reward for one's activity. Just enjoying one's studying seems to be homogeneous with the studying, in a sense not quite the same as that so far described, but it does not seem to be a reward for studying at all. Coming to appreciate contrapuntal music too is obviously homogeneous with this study, and can be called a reward for such study in the way I mentioned earlier (see pp. 4-6).

Now *both* coming to appreciate counterpoint *and* just enjoying its study might be called gaining the 'true reward' of studying counterpoint. So the distinction between instrumental and intrinsic goods does not quite work to explain the notion.

A third feature of the concept of homogeneity and the true reward is this. Someone who studies music just to become rich and famous will often be thought to be missing the point of music, of studying music. This is partly just another way of saying that for him music does not appear as an intrinsically good thing. But obviously it *is* saying this, only if you presuppose that music *is* an intrinsic good. So it is from the musician's point of view that such a man is missing the point. And it is from the musician's point of view that the true reward for studying music is defined, and, indeed, is visible *as* the 'true reward'.

Now the idea that the true reward for any form of activity must be homogeneous with that activity, in the ill-defined sense indicated, is used by Kierkegaard with especial bearing on the *ethical* concept of willing the Good.

If willing the Good (virtue) is rewarded by fame, riches, or even the world's respect and honour, still by the criterion of homogeneity, Kierkegaard believes, we shall be able in these cases only to say that it has been 'apparently' rewarded. For willing the Good, as for anything else, there must be the possibilities both of an apparent reward and of the true reward. And the true reward of willing the Good must be homogeneous with this activity, whatever it is.

Not very helpfully, we might try saying: *any* sort of good may come to a man as a reward for willing the Good. But only some *ethical* (or religious) good could possibly be a candidate for the true reward for this activity, since it is obviously an ethical (or religious) activity.

The line between the 'ethical' and the 'nonethical' is, of course, drawn quite sharply by Kierkegaard. Not that he was the only, or the first, philosopher to do this. Kant, and Plato in the *Gorgias*, both do what comes to the same thing. In particular, all three distinguish sharply between the idea of an 'ethical good' and the idea of a merely 'natural good', examples of which are fame, wealth, and the world's respect.

Thus, for Kierkegaard, no merely natural good can possibly be homogeneous with the ethical act of willing the Good. So the true reward for willing the Good can only be some *ethical* good. Here we cannot help thinking that others have claimed either that virtue is its own reward, or that happiness, in a peculiar sense of the term, is the reward of virtue. Kierkegaard is, I think, getting at both these points.

If there is such a thing as an *ethical* activity, and if such an activity can be described as *truly* rewarded, and if its reward is *homogeneous* with its own (ethical) nature, then there must be some sort of *ethical reward*. And this will describe the true reward for willing the Good.

Kierkegaard provides us with an example, an analogy, for what he is saying. We shall be well advised to consider this example. We are to consider the idea of a young man's loving a girl for the sake of her money. Loving the girl stands to getting a hold over her wealth as willing the Good stands to gaining the appropriate reward—whatever this is conceived to be. So we might call the girl's money the reward for the young man's love. What can be said about this example?

The most striking thing about it is that nearly everybody will feel immediately that something is wrong with this young man. And by and large we shall agree, in general terms, what is wrong: what is wrong is that he has a mercenary attitude towards the girl.

I think this common feeling hides a common conceptualization. For we should quite naturally say that someone like this young man does not *really love* the girl at all. Certainly it does not seem that he loves her for her own sake, for her own charms, for herself! And we find it hard to conceive of anything worth calling 'love' which is not directed upon its 'object' for its object's own sake.

We might put it in this way. For true love, its object must appear an intrinsic good: if its object is merely an instrumental good, then, whatever the appearances, the attitude in question cannot be 'love', but, at most, the appearance of love.

We might put it in another way too. In this example, it looks as though the young man has two things in mind: the girl, and the girl's money, and of the two it is the money which appears to be the operative factor. It is the ultimate end, the goal, of what he does. His loving (or appearing to love) the girl can only be regarded as the means he adopts towards getting her money. (I do not think, however, we need suppose Kierkegaard's example is meant to show us someone of quite this coldly calculating and money-grabbing nature. We need not suppose the young man quite unaffected by or oblivious to the girl's own lovable qualities.)

The distinction between means and end, between instrumental and intrinsic goods, should not be pressed too hard. For we can quite well suppose that for the young man in question the girl herself appears intrinsically desirable. Not all instrumental goods need be purely instrumental; that is, 'good' only insofar as they are means towards purely intrinsic goods. An instrumental good may quite well be seen as itself intrinsically good too. And obviously this adds a great deal to the enjoyment of the pursuit!

Let us, for the time being, suppose that the young man both 'loves' the girl and wants to get her money, and, to remain faithful to the example, that wanting to get her money is his aim or motive in loving her. (There is a pretty obvious strangeness about this last assumption, and I shall return to it at the end of this chapter, pp. 33-36.)

At the least there is supposed to be some kind of connection between his love for the girl and his desire for her money. Now on the plane of psychology we may be able to make sense of this. It is on the plane of values, if I can so speak, that it looks odd. For on the plane of values it is very tempting to say that loving the girl and wanting her money *must* be quite unconnected, or, more probably, opposed. In other words, to value the girl is one thing, to value her money is another. The point is slightly hard to see. It is that, from a certain point of view, such a case must actually involve a kind of *conflict* of values.

Remember here a feature of the concept of the homogeneity of the true reward. It is possible to study music to become rich, disliking music all the while. This is a case where there is no conflict of values, but rather a subordination: something in itself disvalued is given a contingent and instrumental value by being subordinated as the means to something which is positively valued. It is also possible to study music to become rich, but actually to enjoy the music and the study too. This is analogous to the young man's both loving the girl and wanting to get her money. Now contrast this case with the case of someone who studies music for its own sake, not for the money involved, and who perhaps even looks on the possibility of future fame and wealth with dread rather than hope. In this third case, as in the first, there is no conflict of values, since the only thing positively valued is the music: the possibly resulting wealth is seen as an actual disvalue, but as something that must, as it were, be 'risked' for the sake of studying music.

In the second case there are two things valued, and it is this which creates the possibility of a conflict. I say possibility and not necessity, since not all values conflict with one another, and in particular not here. I think it is only from a certain point of view that these two values are seen as conflicting.

We can bring out the nature of this conflict of values by returning to the musician's view of someone who studies music to become wealthy. Now suppose we have here a case of the second kind where the man actually likes music for its own sake. Such a man studies music both for its own sake, and for the sake of the reward—the money to be gained. And the conflict emerges if we ask: how does this man think of the reward for studying music? Obviously he thinks of *both* the enjoyment of studying *and* the financial benefits therefrom as rewards. But this means that he cannot be operating with anything like the conceptual distinction between true and apparent rewards, or the concept of homogeneity.

For someone who, explicitly like Kierkegaard or implicitly like our hypothetical musician, operates with these notions, there must look to be a kind of conflict in such a man's thinking. For he will appear to be treating things of fundamentally heterogeneous kinds as rewards for one and the same activity. And worse: he will appear both to be operating *without* this conceptual apparatus and, implicitly, *with* it. For that he is implicitly operating with the apparatus in question will appear to be shown by his recognition that music is something worth studying for its own sake. For this makes it possible for him too to distinguish between studying music for its own sake (as in case three) and studying merely for the financial rewards (as in case one). And he too, since for him music is something valuable in itself, must see someone who studies music merely for the money as missing at least *that* point about music. I think the same claim can be put more informally thus: to describe somebody as both enjoying the music for its own sake and doing it for the money is to ascribe to him *two conflicting value systems.*

Let us now return to Kierkegaard's young man and his girl. The claim is that, from a certain point of view, to describe the young man as 'loving the girl for the sake of her money' must be to ascribe to him two conflicting systems of values.

How can it be true *both* that he loves the girl for her own sake *and* that he loves her for her money? For on the face of it, to say that he loves her for her money is to deny that he loves her for herself. Intuitively, we seem to be ascribing to this young man a value system oriented, so to speak, around the girl in question, *and* a value system in which the girl appears, if she does appear, only as the appendage of the money, and in which it is the money that plays the central role. (We can imagine the irritation with which Dante would have received such a man's observation that Beatrice was, after all, connected with very wealthy and influential families, and likely to bring with her a considerable dowry.)

Now nobody, and certainly not Kierkegaard, wants to deny that it is possible to fall in love with a girl who also happens to be heiress to a large fortune. That the girl who is the object of your love is wealthy may well be true, but her being wealthy, in this kind of case, is quite external to your love for her.

We might say: although it is true that the girl you love is wealthy, it does not necessarily follow that the object of your love is a wealthy girl. The point can be made by supposing that her father is suddenly bankrupt. If her being an heiress is external to your love for her, then this will not affect your love in the least. Conversely, if it does affect your love, then, *pro tanto*, her being an heiress was not external to your love, and your love was *for* a wealthy girl.

If the young man who loves the girl for her money discovers one day that she has no money, then this discovery must of necessity affect his love for her. If her wealth is the only motive for his love—or 'love'—then, I suppose, he will stop loving her, or pretending to love her. This helps to show the conflict latent in Kierkegaard's description. For insofar as the young man loves the girl for herself, such an event cannot affect his love; while insofar as he loves her for her money, it must affect his love. And his love cannot both be affected and not affected!

Let us consider the notion of a 'reward for one's love'. If a young man falls in love with a girl who happens to be a wealthy heiress, then presumably he may marry her and thus find himself wealthy with her fortune. Now it is not impossible to describe him as being 'rewarded for his love'. I say not impossible, but I do think there is something strange in this description. What is strange is the point of view, the value system, it implies.

One naturally wants to object—and this is the strength of Kierkegaard's example—that whether or not the girl you love is wealthy, beautiful, clever, popular, etcetera, to win her is all the reward you need and all you could have. In comparison with this, finding her to be wealthy, etcetera, is, or should be, as nothing.

One need not despise wealth and beauty for the wealth and beauty of one's wife to be as nothing in comparison with having won her. These things may well provide a genuine pleasure of their own. The 'as nothing' must be taken strictly in the context of one's having loved, wooed, and won the girl. For the question is, what is the good of *just this*? And it is in answering this question that her wealth and beauty do not, or should not, begin to count. From this point of view, nothing like wealth, beauty, popularity, or other values, could possibly begin to count as a 'reward for loving'. We might put this point in the exciting-sounding claim: if by 'reward' is meant wealth or beauty and so forth, then there *cannot be any reward for love.*

This point can be put the other way round. If, on marrying the girl you have wooed and won you discover that she is a wealthy heiress, and if you then see this as the reward for your pursuit, then, from the viewpoint being discussed, that is sufficient to show that it cannot be for *love* you are being rewarded. It shows either that you see yourself as rewarded for something like, say, tenacity or daring—but nothing like 'love'—or that you are simply under an illusion about the true nature of love, if you continue to claim that her wealth is a reward for your 'love'.

Between true love and the object of your love being wealthy or beautiful there can be only a quite external, contingent relation. Insofar as the relation is internal or necessary, your attitude must necessarily have been, whatever you thought, one of avarice, or sexual desire, etcetera. That which can be truly rewarded by money can only be avarice. That which can be truly rewarded by beauty can only be sexual desire, or some kind of aesthetic emotion.

What can truly reward true love?

What can count as a true reward for loving? Surely, as

implied above, only getting the girl, the object of your love. Now this is, I suppose, the answer most people would naturally and unreflectively give. But I do not think it is adequate.

'Getting the girl' might refer to any number of different sorts of outcome. It might mean that she became your pupil, or your client, or your slave, or your prisoner, or your mistress. And if it means 'married her', this too might refer to any number of different sorts of *modus vivendi*. And clearly we want still to draw a distinction between 'valid' and 'invalid' ways of getting the girl. To get her as your slave and keep her as your slave could not, we might object, count as being rewarded for your *love*. For, of course, if you genuinely loved her, you would not want to keep her as your slave!

I suggest that a necessary minimum requirement is this: that you be able to continually express, exercise, and realize your love for the girl. Arriving at a life situation in which you can continually express your love for the girl is, surely something worthy of being called the true reward of love, and the only thing worthy of being called by this name.

We shall obviously have to be careful at this point about the concrete manifestations of this good fortune. For example, marrying her is neither sufficient nor necessary to fulfil the 'formal' requirement so stated. It may even be fulfilled in a way of life in which the girl herself plays no overt part. Dante never 'won' Beatrice in any ordinary sense, yet we want to be able to say that he was *rewarded* for his love for her. For there can be very many different ways of life which express a man's love for someone, and renunciation and sacrifice may well be among them.

Now there is an obvious sense in which the ability (or opportunity) to go on expressing one's love for someone is homogeneous with one's love for that person. Where the reward takes the happy form of winning the girl for a lifetime together, it is simply more of the same—more of the girl and more of one's love! And this is the simplest sort of homogeneity.

This does raise the very difficult question: what is homogeneous with true love? And part of the difficulty is that this, in turn, involves the question: what is the nature of true love? What counts as an expression, an exercise, a realization of true love?

Obviously it is beyond the scope of this inquiry to settle the question of love! But, all the same, I think there is one point which can be indicated here.

I have so far spoken as if the idea of a 'reward for love' can be only the idea of getting the girl (or whatever the object is) you love, and this in the sense of reaching a life situation in which you have continual opportunity for expressing your love. Clearly this description contains two possibly conflicting elements: an element of *getting* and an element of *giving*. These two elements correspond to the two characteristics of love that many philosophers have noticed: that it is partly a kind of desire to get or have and partly a desire to give.

It seems to follow that any 'reward' for love must contain at least elements corresponding to these two characteristics of love. It must be both the gaining of what you desired to get and the giving of what you desired to give.

It is essential, I think, to the concept of 'true love' (and of willing the Good) that it contain these two characteristics, and essential to the concept of its reward that it contain the two corresponding elements. For what can be 'truly rewarded' by mere acquisition, by mere possession, could not be true love, and is hardly to be distinguished from avarice or lust or the drive for power: and what can be truly rewarded by pure giving, by pure sacrifice, although certainly much closer to our concept of love than the former, seems rather to fit the concept of pity or charity or generosity.

Nevertheless the Aristotelian point that love seems much nearer to a kind of giving than a kind of getting is important for this inquiry, and is, perhaps, at the back of Kierkegaard's mind too. Certainly charity—*agape*—has traditionally been seen as a kind of giving, and there is no doubt that Kierkegaard uses this concept as his paradigm for true love (see *Works of Love*, part 1, chapters 2–3 especially).

This is important, too, for its bearing on the notion of a 'reward'. For its immediate bearing is this: the notion of being rewarded for love is *not* the notion of the lover being rewarded by *gaining something*, at least not in the ordinary sense of gain. It is much closer to the idea of the lover being rewarded by giving something to the object of his love.

And what might this 'something' be? I have suggested that it might, in effect, be his love for the loved object: or rather, since 'love' itself cannot be given, the expression, the realizations, and the embodiments of this love.

Of course, the getting-element and the giving-element can hardly be held apart. For somebody who *wants to give* cannot help seeing the opportunity to give, and the giving itself, as *gains*! For certainly he gets what he wants.

Someone whose mind is just on getting things—silver cups, money—for himself, cannot obviously appreciate this kind of situation as a reward. More exactly: someone for whom silver cups are a paradigm of 'rewards' cannot appreciate the opportunity for sacrifice as a reward.

Kierkegaard's example of the young man who 'loves the girl for the sake of her money' bears on the idea of an ethical reward in another way I want to bring out. In bringing this out I shall be contrasting what we might call the 'self-centred' and the 'object-centred' attitudes. And this contrast bears, again, on the distinction between instrumental and intrinsic goods.

The difference between running for the sake of running and running to win a silver cup is commonly expressed by saying that in the former case you are running 'for its own sake', or 'running for the sake of running', whereas in the latter you are running for the sake of the reward. I shall say that the man who runs for the sake of running has an 'object-centred' attitude to his running, and the man who runs to win the cup has a 'self-centred' attitude to his running. (I do not mean a 'selfish' attitude necessarily.)

The man who studies counterpoint simply to become a famous and wealthy conductor differs from the man who studies counterpoint because he loves music (or wants to come to appreciate something he did not previously): the latter studies music for the music's sake, the former does not.

The young man who loves a girl for her money differs from a young man who just loves a girl without considering whether or not she has such things as money, in that the latter's attitude is entirely centred on the girl herself, and the former's is centred on the girl's money—and, moreover, on getting the money for himself.

The point of these contrasts can be brought out, perhaps, if we ask in each case: *whose good* does such a man have in mind? In *whose good* is he interested?

Certainly we shall want to say that the man who runs to win silver cups, like the man who studies counterpoint to become rich, has his own good in mind. And he appears to have a particular conception of 'good'. It is slightly strange to say that the man who runs for the running, or the man who studies music for the music's sake, has the 'good' of the running or the music in mind; but at least we may say that they conceive of the running or the music as (intrinsic) goods in themselves.

The young man who loves a girl for her money obviously has his own good in mind, and moreover conceives it as in some way related to gaining the girl's money.

On the other hand, true love, as I have sketched it out, must involve the idea of the good of the loved one, rather than one's own good. I do not say exclusively. For I want to say that here the two goods are seen as coinciding. And what 'one's own good' comes to is seen as depending on what is the loved one's good.

I said that 'gaining', in true love, may appear from the outside in the guise of giving. It may even appear in the guise of a sacrifice. For if what you desire is the good of the person you love, and if this can be achieved only through your sacrificing your immediate interest in her (him), then such a sacrifice will appear as a gain.

This point should not be expressed by saying that a mark of true love is the lover's willingness to sacrifice his own good for the good of the loved person. For that way of expressing the point implies, and relies on, just that conception of one's own good which I have described as self-centred. There must be room for a conception of one's own good which is not self-centred, but object-centred.

This is the conception which is implied if we put the point thus: a mark of true love is that the lover conceives the good of the loved person *as his own good*. For this implies not that he has *no* conception of his own good, but that his conception of his own good is an object-centred conception.

Now the ideas of 'reward' and 'good' are clearly very closely connected. What I give to somebody as a reward for something, for example, winning a race, must be conceived by me as (in some sense) a good thing for that person to get. For instance, I must suppose that the silver cup is a good thing for the winner to get.

Although the reward must be conceived as a good for the rewardee by the rewarder, it does not follow that the rewardee must see it as good himself. On the contrary, he may think it is quite useless, or disgustingly hideous, or trivial and uninteresting. He may not *feel* rewarded, although, of course, normally he will understand that he has been rewarded, in the conventional sense of receiving something given as a reward.

The same applies where there is no rewarder, for example, in cases like the case where I suddenly come to appreciate a whole area of music I had previously found meaningless.

Importantly, the converse too must be able to occur. It must be possible, for example, for the bystander to observe that I feel myself truly rewarded for my efforts, but for him to disagree—to believe that I have not, in fact, been truly rewarded: that what I have received is not a genuine reward for what I have done.

The young man who loves a girl, without the least concern whether or not she is wealthy, and who finds after marrying her that she is actually heiress to a large fortune, may not see this sudden extra as a reward or, indeed, as a good, in comparison with his having won the girl. But a third party might see the young man as 'rewarded' by the girl's wealth. Or the other way round: the young man might conceive the girl's money as his reward, but the third party think of this as a misconception, or a low conception.

As a man's conception of 'his own good', so his conception of what may reward him. As a man's conception of someone else's good, so his conception of what may reward that person. In particular, if his conception of his own good is someone else's good, or the 'good' of some other thing (running, music), then he must conceive of the good of the other as *his own reward*.

This distinction bears on, but does not coincide with, the distinction between the notions of 'true' and 'apparent' reward introduced earlier. For someone with an 'other-centred' conception of reward may have a conception which is effectively either 'true' or merely 'apparent': the girl's good may be a 'reward' for the young man who loves her ('other-centred'), but he may understand her good either in terms of money, or in some other terms.

Put in another way: one's conception of the reward does not determine one's conception of the nature of the reward, that is, of the good. Being other-centred is not enough to guarantee possessing an exalted conception of the good.

This is why it would be a mistake, I believe, to try to infer from the foregoing arguments that love is a desire for the moral and spiritual good of the loved person. It certainly follows that love is a desire for the good of the loved person, but not, in addition, that this 'good' has to be identified with virtue or blessedness. Nevertheless there seems a strong temptation to say that a mark of true love is its desire for the loved one's virtue or blessedness. But I have not yet been able to see to the sources of this temptation.

The whole example concerning the young man who is alleged to love a girl for her money is intended by Kierkegaard to, and does, throw light on the notion of 'willing the Good for the sake of the reward'. And it is the nature of this illumination that I now want to explore.

Willing the Good is, I said earlier, clearly an ethical conception, and possibly—for Kierkegaard certainly—a religious conception too. But it is not an immediately intelligible conception, and I shall therefore approach it by means of two related conceptions: the idea of loving God and the idea of doing one's duty. (Although I say merely 'related', I am sure that what Kierkegaard means by 'willing the Good' is in fact identical with what would normally be meant by both these ideas.)

About the idea of loving God I shall not say much, and no doubt what I do say will be both banal and inaccurate. We are, presumably, to entertain the idea of a man's purporting to love God for the sake of the rewards to be expected. Now these rewards may be of two kinds: earthly and heavenly.

The idea of a man's purporting to love God for the sake of the earthly rewards to be expected, the natural goods—riches, fame, honour, a long life, health, power, and so forth—to be expected, is clearly strange. For one obvious reason, if earthly rewards are what this man is after, he has adopted an extremely doubtful way of getting them; that is, *if* what is counted as 'loving God' is what is normally so counted.

Worse: in such a man's mind there must be operative *both* the idea of the spiritual good that is God *and* the idea of the natural goods in question. And this raises acutely the problem of homogeneity. As ordinarily understood, natural goods are heterogeneous from spiritual goods. So anyone who shows that for him natural goods might count as the reward for loving God shows thereby that he counts God, or loving God, as some sort of 'natural' activity too—if, indeed, he has any coherent concept of what a true reward means.

The same objection, in a slightly modified form, faces the idea of a man's purporting to love God for the heavenly rewards to be expected, for example, for the sake of the expected joys of Paradise.

This does not mean there is nothing in connecting the idea of 'loving God' with the idea of a reward for loving God, and with the further idea that this reward has something to do with 'joys', that is, with happiness—in some sense of that word.

It is perfectly intelligible to claim that there are rewards for loving God—true rewards—and to name these 'the joys of Paradise', *if* the idea of the joys of Paradise is related to the idea of loving God analogously as the idea of (say) the joys of marriage is related to the idea of loving a girl. This should be expanded, too, to allow for the idea that self-sacrifice may be seen as the reward for such love; that is, that is to be credited with 'joys', a 'happiness', of its own. That is to say: if one's idea of 'winning the joys of Paradise' is the idea of a condition in which one has the ability and opportunity to continually express and realize one's love for God.

This idea will have to be complicated by adding that it is also the idea of a condition in which one *truly* loves God, since theology normally claims that as human beings we do not, here on earth, love God truly, but only, as it were, approximately, partially, and by God's own grace.

Let us turn briefly to the second idea, the idea of doing one's duty, the idea expressed in Luther's, 'I can do no other'. We are, for the example's parallel, to entertain the idea of man's purportedly doing his duty for the sake of the reward.

What is odd about this idea is that such a man appears to have two grounds for doing his duty: one, that it is his duty, and the other, that if he does it, he will (probably) be rewarded for doing it. And we sense a conflict implicit.

It is odd if he himself puts his case in the words 'doing my duty for the sake of the reward'. For, one wants to ask, if he really believes the thing is his duty, what has being rewarded got to do with its performance? Surely if he really believes it is his duty, he must believe he has to do it whether or not he will be rewarded, whether or not there is a reward in the offing. And surely, if he is right in implying that his *reason* for doing whatever it is is just that there is a 'reward' in the offing, he cannot see the action under the heading of 'my duty'?

From a familiar point of view, of course, there is nothing odd in supposing that a man might be induced to do what is in fact his duty, though he does not know this, by the promise of some kind of reward. Again, there is nothing odd in the idea that a man might be given a reward by someone else for having—in the latter's eyes—done his duty; or even, perhaps, for having done what seemed to him his duty.

But with this example the question of distinguishing 'true' from 'apparent' rewards, the question of 'homogeneity' comes to the fore again.

Suppose I do what you believe to have been my duty. You want to reward me, and so you give me, say, a sum of money, or a promotion, or a public address of congratulations. And your giving me this 'good' is backed by the idea in your mind that you are 'rewarding' me for having done my duty, that the good you give me is a 'reward' for my having done my duty.

Now of course I may well be grateful for your gift. And I may see that you intended it as a reward for my having (in your eyes) done my duty. But it does not follow that I have to regard your reward *as* a reward for having done my duty. I may simply think you are mistaken, or influenced by a false conception of values, or a false conception of duty, in believing that anything like (say) money could possibly be an appropriate reward for a man's doing his duty.

From my point of view, your gift is, of course, very pleasant, and it is nice to know that you believe I have done my duty: the only trouble is that it appears that you do not understand what is involved in the concept of a duty. For you obviously think that your reward can and should be taken by me *in the spirit in which it was given*, that is, as a reward.

All this is not to argue that I am correct about the nature of a duty and you are in error. It is simply to argue that our conceptions of duty may well—and sometimes do—differ, in such a way that we may have quite different, and perhaps even mutually contradictory, conceptions of what doing one's duty implies.

If the man's idea, in claiming that he does his duty for the sake of the reward, is that a life of virtue is likely to be accompanied by increasing wealth, fame, honour, and so on, then clearly he does not know much about the world. Virtue can, of course, go with getting on in the world, and it is also possible that this 'getting on' is offered up by the world as a reward to the virtuous man. But, as before, if your heart is set on riches and fame, there are likely to be easier and surer ways of getting these goods than leading a life of virtue. Someone who thinks of virtue, of doing one's duty habitually, in these terms clearly has a very particular conception of 'duty', or 'virtue'. Clearly he does not see it as of intrinsic worth.

'Rewards of virtue' need not refer to earthly goods, like money and fame and happiness, as ordinarily understood. Here we think of something like the joys of Paradise once more. And the point I made about the relation of that idea to the idea of loving God goes also for the relation of this idea of 'rewards of virtue' to the idea of 'virtue', or of 'doing one's duty'.

The ordinary idea of duty (or virtue) is obviously an ethical idea. So nothing can be 'homogeneous' with duty, in the sense discussed earlier, which is not itself defined by an *ethical* concept. This is the fundamental reason why *natural* goods are, just for the reason of their naturalness, heterogeneous from virtue.

But it does not, of course, follow that any and every ethical good is homogeneous, in the required sense, with doing one's duty. For what is peculiar about the latter concept is its containing the idea of moral obligation, or necessity (compare the idea of a categorical imperative).

This is why there is a temptation to think that the very idea of a 'reward for doing one's duty' must necessarily be self-contradictory. But I do not think we have to succumb to this temptation: rather, I think there is a way of looking at these notions for which the idea of a reward for doing one's duty is consistent, though admittedly strange.

Following out the analogy with the case of false and true love, I shall try saying that the idea of a reward for doing one's duty (for virtue) is the idea of a condition in which one has the continual ability and opportunity for doing one's duty.

Of course, from a familiar enough viewpoint this does not sound anything like a 'reward'. And from a familiar viewpoint it sounds like nothing which could be understood as a reward for doing one's duty, since it just is, as it were, more of the same— more doing one's duty. And from this familiar point of view a 'reward' has at least necessarily to be distinct from that which is being rewarded.

But I have been arguing, throughout this chapter, that there may be a point of view, or a system of values, from which these familiar beliefs appear inadequate. And Kierkegaard's position seems to be an instance of such a point of view.

One further point should be raised here, though no more than raised. It concerns the idea of freedom in its connection with the idea of morality, that is, with the idea of doing one's duty, virtue, and 'willing the Good'.

There is an oddity in the very idea of a 'reward for love', in the idea of the young man's loving the girl for the sake of her money. And the oddity comes from an implicit contradiction in this idea.

The contradiction is roughly as follows. The idea of 'doing something for the sake of something else' implies the idea of doing that thing intentionally. But the ordinary idea of 'loving some-body' is the idea of something done or incurred *not* intentionally. Or rather, the very joining of these two concepts seems to produce an absurdity: the absurd notion of 'intentionally loving'. It is such an absurd notion that is implied in the idea of loving a girl *for the sake of* her money or anything else.

In general, the idea 'for the sake of' fails to produce absurdity *only* when joined with the idea of something which we can think of as being done 'intentionally'.

The reason why its conjunction with the idea of love, as ordinarily understood, produces absurdity is that the idea of love is the idea of something *spontaneous*. For we ordinarily think of love as being some kind of emotional state or condition, and the emotions are certainly conceived as states or conditions which come upon one 'spontaneously'. One's will and intentions are not and cannot be involved in the bringing about of such conditions.

There is something else. Although the idea of the girl's money cannot be understood as a reason for (or as a cause of) the young man's love for her, there are certain other conditions and activities it can be so understood for. The idea of her money can quite well be understood as the *cause* of the young man's desire to get hold of this money. And also as the *reason* for his attempts to get hold of it, for example, by wooing and marrying her. (I do not wish to imply any particular doctrine about the relations between the concepts 'cause' and 'reason'.)

This is probably why, when faced by the purported claim that the young man *loves* the girl for the sake of her money, we are apt to construe this as a misleading way of expressing the claim that he is acting as if he loved the girl, whether consciously or under the illusion that he really does love her, with the aim of getting hold of her money—this aim, too, being conscious or 'unconscious'.

Now this feature of the ordinary idea of love is analogous to a certain feature of the conception of 'doing one's duty'. The analogy is that this conception of doing one's duty is also the conception of something which cannot be *caused*.

The analogy has to be worked out rather carefully. It is not that love cannot be caused: if thought of as something like an emotional condition, it most probably will be thought of as *ipso facto* something which can be caused, though the causes of a man's falling in love will be obscure. But at least some kinds of agency are fairly definitely excluded from the range of possible *causes for love*. And among these will be, for example, the belief that the girl in question is wealthy. Whatever emotional condition this belief may induce, we are not ordinarily prepared to consider that it might be genuine love, although it may bear quite a number of the external marks of love.

Generalizing, we might say that no belief that there is a reward in the offing could, as ordinarily conceived, count as a possible cause for a man's genuinely *loving* someone. (Remember that we have already excluded the possibility of there being anything that could count as a *reason* for the man's love.)

Again, there is a lack of similarity between being in love and doing one's duty in another important respect: whereas the former is conceived as something which it is absurd to suppose 'intentional', the latter is ordinarily conceived as something which must necessarily be supposed to be intentional. Still, the same feature goes for a man's intentions in (reasons for) doing his duty as goes for the causes of a man's love; namely, that in neither case can the idea of the 'reward' count.

There is another way of bringing out this analogy. In the cases both of love and of the will to do one's duty, a man must be supposed to have some idea of, some beliefs about, the object of his love or his will. It is these beliefs, or a selection from them, that constitute what philosophers often call the 'intentional object' of his mind.

The point, briefly, is that neither in the case of love nor in the case of the will to do one's duty can the idea of the object of one's love or will figure under the aspect of 'likely to bring a reward with it'. And it is partly to this idea that I was referring earlier, when I discussed the application of the instrumental intrinsic distinction to our problem.

CHAPTER 2   Illness and 'fearing what one should fear'

P arallel to the idea of 'willing the Good for the sake of the reward' is the idea of 'willing the Good out of fear of the punishment' (*Purity of Heart*, pp. 79–98). For this is willing the Good 'for the sake of avoiding the punishment'.

Parallel, not, of course, identical. So that we should not expect that everything of logical or ethical interest in the former idea is also to be found in the latter. But we may reasonably expect them to share at least some common peculiarities. And we may expect that, even where the peculiarities of these two ideas diverge, an analysis of one will tend to illuminate possible peculiarities in the other. Much of what I said in the first chapter will, therefore, probably be repeatable in some altered form apropos of the idea of 'willing the Good out of fear of the punishment'. This would be a somewhat mechanical operation. So I do not intend to perform the transformation. Instead, I will explore some novel points made by Kierkegaard.

'Willing the Good out of fear of the punishment' may be called a kind of *conditional* willing of the Good. It is a kind of willing whose maxim, using a Kantian terminology, could have only the logical form of a hypothetical imperative, but not the form of a categorical imperative.

To describe someone as willing the Good 'out of fear of the punishment', or 'for the sake of avoiding the punishment', is to imply that, if he did not believe a failure to will the Good would be punished, he would not be willing the Good, or, at least, not intentionally so (a strange concept!).

It implies, in fact, that it is because he believes this—and *only* because he does—that he wills the Good. This is the reason why he wills the Good; his reason for so doing. Thus, if the 'condition of the will' is absent, so will the willing be too, as far as this description goes, at least.

In part, Kierkegaard's further analyses and analogies are attempts to bring out the force of this implication, and in particular to show that it means that the original description contains a latent absurdity by implicitly contradicting itself. For Kierkegaard believes that the idea of 'willing the Good' is the idea of something which could not be done conditionally, that is, for the sake of achieving some further goal. Willing the Good cannot name an activity which is performed merely as the *means* to some further end.

This general point seems to lie behind, and to give general logical force to, many of the particular points about the idea of 'willing the Good out of fear of the punishment' which Kierkegaard goes on to make.

I wish here to cite three passages from Plato's *Gorgias* (479D–480B). Plato, or rather Socrates, here expresses a view of morality which is in many respects very close to the view I believe Kierkegaard is arguing for. (This was pointed out by Peter Winch in his paper 'Can A Good Man Be Harmed?', *Proc. Arist. Soc.*, 1965–66.) These citations may help to focus the discussion that is to follow.

> 1 / Wrongdoing, then, is merely the second greatest of evils; to do wrong and not to be punished is the greatest and the first of all evils.
>
> 2 / It must, then, follow from what we have agreed that a man must guard himself closely, so as not to do wrong. . . .
>
> 3 / And if either he or anyone he cares for does wrong, he must himself willingly go to where he will be punished as fast as possible, to the judge, as to the doctor. . . .

When a man purports to will the Good for the sake of avoiding the punishment, this can be only because he wants to avoid the punishment, and this only because he fears the punishment. (When a man wills the Good for the sake of the reward, this can be only because he *hopes* for the reward.)

Kierkegaard will not try to argue that the concept of 'fear' is irrelevant to the concept of 'willing the Good', or that it distorts the latter. For he himself believes, as does Socrates (see second citation from Plato) that fear has something important to do with willing the Good. But he believes that the right way of bringing out this connection is quite different, both logically and psychologically, from the way it is brought out in the purported 'willing the Good out of fear of the punishment'.

Roughly, as a preliminary and guiding notion, we can say that for Kierkegaard there are two ideas of 'fear', or two kinds of fear, that one may wish to show related to the idea of willing the Good. There is the idea of the fear a man may reasonably feel when contemplating the idea of a punishment that is liable to fall upon him for any failure to will the Good. And there is the quite different idea of the fear a man might feel when contemplating the idea that he is liable to fail to will the Good. One might also call this 'fear of the Good'.

Kierkegaard will try to argue, by means of an extended analogy among other things, that there is something dangerously confused about the former idea, something dangerously wrong about that kind of fear, that kind of reason for fear. Indeed, such fear is seen as evidence for a wrong understanding of morality.

Paradoxically, from the ordinary point of view, that attitude which evidences a right understanding of morality is not *fear* at the idea of being punished for failure to will the Good. It is a kind of satisfaction, or even, I think, a kind of *hope*. The wrongdoer ought not to fear his punishment: he ought to desire it. That is, he ought to *hope* for punishment (see the third citation from Plato).

We are to consider an extended analogy, or series of analogies, of which two are particularly relevant. These are the analogy between moral goodness and health; and the no doubt implied analogy between the punishment for wrongdoing, and medicine, or, more generally, the cure for illness.

It is, perhaps, not necessary to stress the *individual* analogies too much. It is probably necessary only to stress the analogies of *structure*. For example, we may not need to construe Kierkegaard as conceiving moral goodness as a condition of the soul analogous to that bodily condition called 'health'. We may need only to claim that he saw an analogy between the relations between illness, medicine, and health on the one hand, and the relations between wrongdoing, punishment, and moral goodness on the other — or, more precisely, an analogy between the relations between these respective concepts.

Now one may well fear either wrongdoing or its punishment. In the case we are analysing it is clearly a fear of punishment that is predominant. If punishment stands to wrongdoing as medicine (cure) stands to illness, then the fear of punishment, in the ethical realm, is analogous to the fear of medicine (cure) in the physical realm.

The fear of the cure is, in effect, a fear of getting well. For we may suppose that the cure is the only possible means of getting well. So fearing the cure is fearing what (one recognizes) is necessary in order to get well. Now obviously one may be justified in fearing a particular cure, since it may be extremely painful. This is not in question. But if one's fear of the cure is so great as to prevent one determining to submit to the cure for the sake of getting well, then we shall have to say that the cure is feared more than the health is desired. And that is to say: the cure is regarded as a greater evil than the health is regarded as a good, so that the evil of the cure outweighs the good of the health. This is one oddity about such an outlook.

Further, we seem to have a case of confusion between instrumentality and intrinsicality of 'good' and 'evil'. We may suppose that the state of health is regarded as a good in itself, as intrinsically good. (This does not prevent its being regarded also as instrumentally good, but this aspect of its concept does not play a part in the deliberation we are analysing.)

Now ordinarily a 'cure' would be regarded as good, insofar as it can be conceived as good, only insofar as it brings about the good state of health, that is, only as instrumental in bringing about something that is good in itself. It would be admitted, normally, that in itself the cure may be hardly good at all, or not good at all, but just an evil.

But in thinking of the cure as a means to health, this aspect of the cure would ordinarily and properly be considered irrelevant, except, perhaps, in weighing the desirability of alternative possible cures. That the cure is *in itself* an evil has not the least tendency to show that it is *as an instrument* evil (or useless), nor, more strongly, is it in any way relevant to the question of its being *as an instrument* good or bad.

If one were simply thinking in means-end terms about getting well, then only one 'intrinsic good' (or evil) could possibly enter one's deliberations; namely, the intrinsic good of the state of health. The other goods and evils that enter one's deliberation could only be instrumental; that is, they could only enter one's deliberation under the form of their instrumentality for goodness or evil.

To be considering the cure under the form of its intrinsic good or evil is then *not* to be just thinking in means-end terms about getting well. It is to have a second form of thought in one's mind at the same time.

Further, both systems of thought involve values, that is, intrinsic goods. Thus there is a latent conflict of value, a conflict of two different value systems, in such a man's mind. For in one such system the idea of the cure appears necessarily *not* under its form as intrinsic value, but in the other it appears necessarily only under its form as intrinsic value. So we may say of such a man that he is thinking inconsistently or, less intellectually put, that he is simultaneously operating in two incompatible value systems.

There is another point about this sort of case. It concerns a possible difference between the kinds of good or evil involved.

Well-being, or health, is a good, and so of course is pleasure: illness is an evil and so is pain. (The logical status of these assertions does not concern me here.)

In the ordinary kind of case, a man who fears to be cured is afraid of the pain that the cure involves. But this is not a necessary truth and is not necessarily implied in the general argument I am unfolding. It will do to illustrate this second point.

Normally, though maybe not necessarily, illness involves pain and health involves pleasure. But one may value health, even if it involves pleasure, for other reasons than that it involves pleasure. (Of course, if it does not necessarily involve pleasure, one must value health for other reasons.)

It is quite conceivable, on the other hand, that a man might value health only insofar as it involved pleasure. This might lead to his not valuing health when it did not involve pleasure, if there are such possibilities. We might say that such a man has a 'hedonistic' attitude to the value of health. This might well be part of a more general, or perhaps universal, hedonism on such a man's part.

If the cure is regarded under its aspect as painful, and if the state of health that is to result is regarded under its aspect as pleasant, then in an obvious sense there is a 'homogeneity' of values in the case. But if the state of health is regarded as a value for some reason other than that it involves pleasure, it may be possible to say that the values of the cure and the health are 'heterogeneous'. Possible, although perhaps not necessary. For it may appear impossible to compare, in respect of their intrinsic values, the cure and the state of health.

The cure and the health might well appear to be values, or goods, of quite different kinds. And it might appear that only the cure could be regarded as a value of the kind we may call 'hedonic'.

For someone who sees the cure and the resulting health in some such way as this, a man whose fear of the cure stands in the way of his offering himself up to it will appear to be making two mistakes, under two confusions at once. One will be the confusion between the cure as instrumentally and as intrinsically valuable. The other will be the confusion between the nature or kind of the cure's intrinsic value, that is, its being pleasant, and the intrinsic value of the resulting state of health.

This example must be carefully distinguished from a case which is possible but not the kind in question. It might be held that a man whose fear of the cure prevented his seeking it, and so prevented his getting well again, overvalued the pain — or other evils — involved in the cure in relation to the good, however identified, of the resulting health. This would perhaps be a kind of 'disproportion' in his appreciation of these values.

The objection that a man was too afraid of the pain, in comparison with the goodness of the state of health resulting from the cure, might be made. But it is very different from the kind of objection I have been discussing. For it presupposes the 'homogeneity' of the values of the cure and the state of health, whereas precisely one of the two points of objection I have been discussing is that these values should be regarded as 'heterogeneous'.

It is not that the man who will not undergo the cure out of fear of the pain fears the pain too much in comparison with the good of the resulting health. It is, rather, that, from a certain point of view, there may seem to be no comparison possible between the pain and the good of the health. This is not to say that, from this point of view, the pain of the cure is not seen as in any way an evil. In itself it may be regarded as just as great an evil from this point of view as from the purely hedonistic point of view.

It is, rather, that part of what constitutes this point of view is that when health or illness are in question, when the deliberation concerns these particular values, the idea of the cure (medicine) can come up only in the form of an instrumentality. So the idea of the intrinsic value of the cure cannot come up at all in such deliberation.

The idea of a man's fearing the cure is clearly meant to exemplify the idea of a man's fearing what he should not fear. What exemplifies the idea of a man's not fearing what he should fear will, clearly, be the idea of a man's not fearing the illness, or a man's not fearing illness in general. This is the analogue, in the physical realm, of the idea, in the ethical realm, of a man's not fearing wrongdoing, or not fearing that condition of the self (soul) from which wrongdoing flows.

What sense can we give to the claim that a man who does not

fear illness does not fear what one should fear?

Notice first that there does not seem to be an 'if' involved in this claim. It looks—and is used by Kierkegaard—as though it exemplified some notion of what a man should fear *tout simple*, unconditionally, absolutely, and independently of any further and distinct aims to be gained by so doing.

We can make sense of this, I think, if we think of the ideas of life and death in a particular way. (This is probably the ordinary common-sense way too.) That is, if we think of birth and death as the termini of human life. Maybe we do not have to go as far as saying they are the termini of all life. Still, the kind of life outside these termini will not be intelligible as a 'human life'— the kind of existence there will not be the existence of a human being, a person, as we ordinarily understand this idea.

The idea of illness obviously stands closely related to the idea of death. So the idea of fearing illness stands closely related to the idea of fearing death.

Now by 'illness' we do not, I think, have to understand just the kinds of *disease* treated by medicine. For the purpose of the argument, we can take it as covering physical harm in general, or physical defect in general.

Physical harm and death are obviously related ideas, in that physical harm covers one genus of cause of death in human beings. And physical defect and life are related ideas in another way, too. For in the sense of 'life' in which life involves activity and its possibility, physical defect covers one genus of cause of the inability to lead a human life.

Fearing 'illness', in this extended sense, amounts then to fearing that physical harm which tends in general to cause death, and to fearing that physical defect which tends in general to lessen the capacity to lead a human life—a human existence. 'Health', understood in the same sense, will be that physical well-being and perfection which enables a man to live a complete, or adequate, human life.

So fearing illness, thus understood, will be fearing what tends to lessen one's capacity for — or maybe remove — human existence, that is, for acting out what one is (namely, a human being). Conversely, desiring or hoping for health, so understood, will simply be desiring that physical condition which sustains one's capacity for such an existence.

I have been talking as if the ideas of illness and health were the ideas of conditions which are conditions for the human existence or its absence. This sounds like saying they are ideas of a certain kind of *means* to living the human life, that is, implying that the latter idea functions to signify the unconditional *end* in our ordinary thinking.

But I do not want to imply reliance on the means-end category in my discussion of the idea of illness. For the illness can be understood as an idea which is related not externally but *internally* to the ideas of death and life. For example, losing a leg may be conceived as *preventing* a man's being an athlete, and in this way as a kind of 'causal' antecedent of his subsequent condition. But the relationship between being without one leg and not being capable of athletic feats is not just a contingent one!

This discussion may help to show why one might want to claim that the fear of illness is a fear of what one should fear, a fear that one should possess; or, conversely, that the desire for health is a desire for what one should desire, a desire that one should possess. For not to possess such fear (such hope) is not to possess a fear of death, and not to possess a desire for human life.

This is, in a broad sense, a matter of one's system of values. I say broad sense, since it is not necessarily moral values, still less religious ones, that need be implied.

Not to possess the normal desire for human life is not to regard this life as a good thing. (One may desire other things more than life, and this possibility is cardinal to Kierkegaard's whole position. But that of itself would not imply not desiring this life at all.)

But if a man does not value human existence, taken in this wide sense, one may well wonder what on earth he does value or what on earth he can value. Not to desire human life, that is, not to see it as a good, appears to imply not seeing anything within the scope of this life as a good, or not seeing anything 'natural' as a good. (I realize the difficulty of this way of expressing the matter.)

For someone for whom human life is the be-all and end-all, that which contains all possibilities of action and desire for human beings, all human goods and evils, the idea of 'life' has a peculiar limiting function. It would be wrong, I think, to say that such a man needs to conceive life as no more than a, or the, *means* to achieving or even perceiving the (natural) goods. The ideas are related more intimately than that.

Now I do not want to claim that this analogy is perfect. There is at least one very important point at which it fails to represent something typically 'ethical' in the claim that a man should fear wrongdoing. To say that the fear of illness (death), that is, the valuing of life, is something a man 'should' possess is, as I have tried to argue, to imply that there is something categorical or *unconditional* about the demand that life be seen as a good: this does resemble a similar feature in the ethical claim. But, still, the unconditionality of the demand that (from the natural point of view) life be seen as a good is not an *ethical* unconditionality. In other words, this demand is not an ethical demand.

If a man does not see his life as a good, then one may well wonder what on earth he does, or can, see as a good. And one may conclude that there can be nothing on earth that he can see as a good. (I have allowed for his being, on the other hand, a religious individual and have, therefore, distinguished this case.) But in this discussion nothing has been implied about what, ethically speaking, he should see as a good, about what he morally ought to fear or hope for.

The idea that a man who does not fear death does not fear what a man *should* fear is not the idea that he does not fear what it is his moral duty or responsibility to fear. It is the idea that he does not fear what is unconditionally demanded of any man that he fear, where the demand is made not by morality, or God, but by something more like prudence, or reason, or nature.

These are puzzling ideas, and it is very possible that there is something implicitly self-contradictory in the development of the idea I have tried to trace. If so, that will be the very point at which the *ethical* analogy breaks down. But there is one more point — or maybe an aspect of the same point — which may help to bring out the force of this analogy.

Not valuing, or not thinking intrinsically good, one's human life can be part of several different world-views. One is the view of the religious man for whom everything in this world is nothing. This attitude is quite distinct from the attitude of the man for whom everything in this world is nothing in comparison with the good things of eternity. For the latter may well think the goods of the world, and therefore its life too, are of very great value — in those terms appropriate to such goods. Though not in terms appropriate to the goods of the next world, that is, 'eternity'.

Another is the world-view, if it can be so called, of the man for whom everything is nothing. I do not know if such an attitude is ever sane. I doubt it. There might be a case where a man has lost absolutely everything on which he had previously put any high value, for instance, his marriage and his family, his employment, his physical capacities, his contentment and stability of mind, his health, and his financial support. It might not be too surprising to hear a man in such a case say that he would prefer to be dead, or say that living no longer meant anything to him. Such things are sometimes heard from the mouths of people who are suicidally depressed even for lesser reasons, or apparently lesser ones.

These 'exceptions' support my argument. For they tend to show that it is scarcely conceivable that anyone should not be thought to place a value on his continued life, if he does not occupy one of these extreme existential positions — if he is not religious, or suicidal, or just insane.

I think, in fact, it would not be too daring to suppose that part of what is ordinarily considered to define and constitute a 'normal' outlook on life, that is, an outlook which is neither insane nor psychologically deformed *nor involves religion*, is that the idea of life itself must take the limiting and central (architectonic) place in the system of values corresponding to that outlook. The italicized qualification is not meant to imply that a religious outlook either is or is not ordinarily thought abnormal. Perhaps it is, perhaps it is not. I am here considering the idea of human existence, life in this world, as it appears to somebody who acknowledges that he is living in this world, and that this existence is not just nothing at all to him.

Remember that throughout I have been talking entirely in natural terms, in the terms of the 'natural' man. This means that I am not talking in religious terms, or of possible religious outlooks on life and death; nor in ethical terms of possible ethical attitudes to life and death.

Indeed by completely omitting these factors, I hope that I have to some extent brought out what is involved in an 'ethical' or 'religious' attitude to human life and death, in a negative kind of way. For the most obvious comment from either point of view is likely to be: but ethically (or, religiously) speaking, natural life and death do not necessarily appear to count at all! For example, we want, I think very naturally, to allow for the possibility and meaningfulness of self-sacrifice, the sacrifice of one's life, either within an ethical or (more clearly) within a religious outlook. These are the very points Kierkegaard is, I think, trying to hint at.

Let us return to the puzzling idea of a man's not fearing what he should fear and try to clarify it by making certain conceptual distinctions. 'Not fearing what it is reasonable to fear' might mean any one of several things. (1) We might wish to say, by using this form of words, that the man in question was rash, that is, he habitually exposed himself to unwarranted dangers. This would be a kind of foolishness. (2) But we might wish to imply, further, that his apparent 'rashness' was in fact the effect of *ignorance*, that is, ignorance of dangers. This would not be foolishness. (3) And we might want to indicate that the man was in some way defective as regards such normal emotions of fear and panic. This attitude, too, would be neither a kind of foolishness, nor a kind of ignorance, but rather a kind of 'stolidity'.

1 / In the first case, we are charging the man with a lack of *prudence*. He does not *do* what it is prudent, reasonable, to do in the face of danger. Now we have to distinguish this from the exhibition of *courage*, which may well also involve not doing what it is prudent to do in the face of danger. To see a man as acting *rashly* is precisely not to see him (among other things) as acting *courageously*. Courage is not a form of imprudence: exhibiting courage is not acting unreasonably, without sense.

Of course the same behaviour in the same circumstances that I regard as courageous you may regard as merely rash. (All this too is in Aristotle.) What is the difference between these concepts?

To see a man's behaviour as courageous is to find it praiseworthy. Courage is a form of 'good behaviour'—speaking vaguely enough. Certainly the idea of goodness is closely related to the idea of courage. I think it is related in two different ways. To ascribe courage to a man implies ascribing to him a *good will*; that is the appreciation of some state of affairs as *good in itself* and the aim to bring this state of affairs to pass by means of the activity we see as exhibiting courage. It implies that the man has some *end* in view in his so acting and that he sees this as an intrinsic good. To ascribe courage to a man also implies that I, the observer and judge of his behaviour, find something good in the situation. This 'good' might simply be the fact of the man's good will, but ordinarily involves my appreciating as intrinsically good the very same end which I ascribe to the man in question.

To see a man's behaviour as rash is to find it unpraiseworthy, thought not, I think, to find it blameworthy — not necessarily, at least. The idea of goodness is related here too, but obviously in a different way from the way it relates to courage. Maybe there is nothing in the case which he thinks, or I think, intrinsically good. So either there is no good reason for him to be behaving as he is, or I cannot see that there is. So it appears that he is *just* risking his life, or his money, to no purpose.

Now it is not necessary to see such a case in terms of the idea of 'rashness', or in terms of a stress on the notion of 'just' risking whatever is being risked, or in terms of the idea of a 'risk' as something which there is no point in undergoing for its own sake. For it is possible to have a view of life in which the idea of a risk plays, so to speak, a positive part, and not the negative part it ordinarily plays in our thinking.

In such a view of life the idea of danger plays a similarly positive, and so unusual, part. This is a view of life which might be, roughly, described by saying that, instead of conceding to ordinary common sense, or prudence, some sort of worth, and far from regarding it as a kind of virtue, one regards it as something positively undesirable. As a quality of character which a man would be better for lacking. As signifying, perhaps, an unduly 'mean', or materialistic, or self-centred system of values. There are clearly various possibilities here.

Loosely, we might describe such views of life as views in which danger is seen not as *dangerous* — or not merely as dangerous — but as exciting, or demanding, or inspiring, or challenging. (That view of life in which danger is seen as unavoidable in all human enterprises is not quite the same.)

Many other concepts will no doubt appear in such a view of life with very different faces — very different applications — from those they wear ordinarily. Among them, importantly, is the concept of courage. There is a certain resemblance between the way a man whose view of life this is takes the idea of courage, and the way the 'rash' man of Aristotle's *Ethics* takes it. For both, what is ordinarily regarded as courageous behaviour will be less striking than it is ordinarily found to be.

The idea of rashness has a second aspect which bears on my

discussion. The idea of goodness may be connected with this idea in a second way. For behaviour may be seen as rash, not because no good can be appreciated in the situation or the agent's apprehesion of it, but because the observer finds a *disproportion* in the situation. This is a disproportion between two goods, or between the values of two elements in the situation. It is a disproportion between the good at which the rash behaviour aims, and the good which it jeopardizes or risks. For, generally, if the good at which a man's behaviour aims seems significantly less than the good which it jeopardizes, his behaviour is likely to be seen as rash.

This concept of proportion applies, obviously, in connection with the concept of courage. Here, by contrast with the case of rashness, it seems that identifying behaviour as courageous implies *not* that no risk is involved, not that nothing is risked or that no good is jeopardized, but that the good aimed at is not disproportionately small.

Interestingly, it implies also, I believe, that the good aimed at is not disproportionately great. For if it were so much greater than the good placed at risk, then it would be hard to distinguish the man's behaviour from prudence, or something like it. In the idiom, he would be 'on to a good thing'.

We must be careful to distinguish this idea of 'proportion' from the idea of 'homogeneity' I introduced in the first chapter. Obviously it is not enough for two goods to be conceived as proportionate that they be conceived as homogeneous. Yet it is also certain that two goods could not bear any proportion or any ratio to each other unless they were homogeneous, in at least the minimum sense of being comparable as to intrinsic value. This distinction, and the introduction of the concept of homogeneity, adds complications to the analysis I have so far given.

The concepts of courage, rashness, and their ilk, are in part explained in terms of the concept of danger and its kin, for example, the concepts of harm and injury.

To conceive of something or some situation as 'dangerous' is to conceive of it as a *threat* to some *good* — to something or some condition thought valuable in particular respects. Examples of things ordinarily considered dangerous are things which are normally thought to threaten one's life, limbs, bodily welfare, health, etcetera. So these are examples of the kinds of thing ordinarily considered valuable in the relevant respects—examples of the kinds of good to which the concept of danger applies. One might call these 'natural' or 'material' goods. Then it will go easily to say that the ordinary concept of danger, which is partly defined by reference to these goods, is a concept of 'natural' danger or 'material' danger.

It is obvious—analytic—that something can be a 'danger' in respect of some good only if it is homogeneous with that good. In respect of the natural goods of bodily welfare, for example, it is obvious that only 'bodily', that is, physical, things and events can constitute danger. For only they can possibly 'threaten' one's bodily welfare.

We have, then, I think, to distinguish the *disproportion* which marks rashness off from courage or prudence from the *heterogeneity* which makes it impossible to establish any kind of relation between the respective worths of the good jeopardized and the good aimed at.

An example may illustrate this distinction. Suppose a man risks his life for the sake of his faith. Now there are at least three possible ways of taking this case. One person might regard this action as rash, perhaps on the grounds that the improbability of his faith being true rendered any possible goods to be gained through martyrdom themselves improbable of achievement. In effect, he sees the man as staking all for little or nothing. Another person might consider that the nature of that good which is our natural life, and the nature of that (admitted) good which is our salvation—our eternal life—are so distinct that they are incomparable. In effect, no question of 'prudence' or 'imprudence' can then arise. And a third person, of course, might see these goods as comparable, and judge the man's action either merely prudent, in view of the 'infinite' superiority of one to the other, or courageous. (There are other possible reactions too.)

2 / So far I have discussed some aspects of the idea of a man's not fearing what it is reasonable to fear, where this concept is understood in the light of the idea of rashness as opposed to prudence, or courage. I turn now, briefly, to consider the same idea understood in the light of the idea of ignorance as opposed to knowledge, or appreciation.

A man may be unafraid of something, or some kind of thing, simply because he does not know, and cannot see, that it is dangerous. In the ordinary case of this sort, what happens is that the man is enlightened, either by somebody else or by his own actual experience, of the thing's dangerous (harmful) qualities. And in this way he comes to have a healthy fear for the thing.

'Dangerous' does not here, or ordinarily, imply a liability to cause just any sort of harm. Mostly it means physical harm, and within this range the harm has to be 'considerable' with respect to the powers of the being harmed: for instance, an electric fire is dangerous to an infant, although it would be odd to say that it was a dangerous thing without qualification.

Ordinarily one comes to appreciate the actual characteristics, tendencies, habits, and qualities of the thing in relation to oneself, that is, one's own capacities for being harmed. To appreciate these things is enough to understand that, and why, it is dangerous. Of course, it is also necessary to learn just what one's capacities are for being harmed, for example, to what degree one's skin can be punctured or slashed, one's bones broken, or one's desires perverted. Generally, and roughly speaking, we learn what constitutes 'harm' through experience and generalization from experience.

Physical harm is obviously something more easily and generally experienced, and so appreciated, than the other forms of harm, for instance, psychological harm, or moral harm (if any), or spiritual harm (again, if any). And I suppose that physical harm is the first kind to be appreciated, and thus remains in some manner 'paradigmatic' for all other kinds of harm, or for all other senses of harm.

It is not ordinarily doubted, or questioned, that it is possible to *know* what constitutes harm, and that certain kinds of thing tend to cause harm and are therefore harmful. Some philosophers have questioned an implication of this ordinary view, but I do not intend to discuss their views. Nor do I intend to raise the question of the grounds for judging that something has caused *harm*, that is, of the objective basis for such judgements, if any. Ordinarily, I think, we define the idea of harm by reference to the ideas of pain and incapacitation, and ordinarily we agree, although not necessarily always or universally, on what sorts of bodily conditions fall under these ideas.

If there were an analogy in this respect between the idea of physical harm and the idea of, say, psychological harm, it would follow that we ordinarily consider the latter idea in the light of the ideas of 'psychological pain' and 'psychological incapacitation'. Now roughly enough this suggestion seems correct. We certainly do have notions of such states as grief, sorrow, depression, melancholy, and boredom on the one hand, and inhibition, timidity, nervousness, fear, and weakness of the will on the other: such notions seem to fall quite naturally under the two general headings I introduced. It is no doubt largely because these ideas are in themselves less clearly defined that it is less easy to say clearly, or to reach agreement on, what constitutes psychological harm.

There is another important difference, too. Even if psychological states like depression were as easily identified as physical conditions of pain and injury, it would still be less easy and natural to identify them as kinds of *harm* than it is to identify such physical conditions as harm.

This is because it is less easy to identify that condition of being *unharmed* by reference to which harm is visible. It is harder to say what constitutes the natural, normal, healthy condition of the mind than to say what constitutes the natural condition of the body.

The idea of 'harm' is in part defined by reference to the ideas, vaguely enough understood, of 'good' and 'bad' or 'evil', of 'right' and 'wrong', and even of 'ought not'. And what conditions of the mind count as psychological *goods*, or as the *right* conditions of the mind, or as those conditions in which the mind *ought* to stand, are questions much less easily answered than the corresponding questions about conditions and physical goods.

This is truer still with respect to the ideas of 'moral harm' and 'moral good', and 'spiritual harm' and 'spiritual good'.

3 / There is a great deal of very great importance that I have not been able to say here on these topics. I now turn briefly to consider the idea of a man's not fearing what it is reasonable to fear, in the light of the idea of emotional stolidity.

This is the quite simple idea that some people are less liable to particular, or general, emotional disturbances than other people are. It is an analogue of the simple idea that some people feel less pain in particular circumstances than others do; for example, some people are not *hurt* by hot things as readily as are others.

Obviously, since fear functions largely to protect us from harm, the man whose capacities for fear are smaller than usual, but whose capacities for being harmed are the same as usual, is more likely to be harmed than most of us are. In this sense, emotional stolidity is a danger.

But this condition of the emotions is obviously something we can hardly conceive of as the individual's 'fault', nor indeed as in any way within his control. He cannot increase his emotional sensitivity nor decrease it. So, in this respect, the very idea of 'what it is reasonable to fear' may fail to apply in this area. For the idea of 'how much it is reasonable to fear' certainly seems to fail to apply.

Nonetheless, it still makes sense, I believe, to conceive such a man as lacking something which every human being *needs*, and in this sense *ought* to possess. It makes sense to suppose that human beings need to be capable quite generally of fear in some situations; and perhaps to suppose also that there are some kinds of things which all human beings need, and in this sense, ought, to fear.

Now obviously 'need' in this sense might well be called 'conditional'. If one asks why all human beings need such a capacity, the answer can only, it seems, be given by describing what good, that is, what use, the capacity for fear is to a human being. What use it is in a human life: what, in such a life, it is needed for: what goods of this human life it is needed for preserving or achieving, and what evils (harms) needed for averting.

CHAPTER 3

The idea of punishment in morality

'T'he man who only wills the Good out of fear of punishment does not will one thing. He is double-minded' (*Purity of Heart*, p. 79).

Let us consider the meaning of Kierkegaard's claim.

He begins by distinguishing two 'spiritual illnesses': one, described as 'not fearing what one should fear', that is, not fearing to do wrong; the other, described as 'fearing what one should not fear, that is, fearing the punishment for wrongdoing.

If wrongdoing, or the state from which wrongdoing flows, is analogous in the spiritual (for example, religious or ethical) realm to the illness, and the punishment for wrongdoing is analogous to the cure, the medicine, then these two spiritual illnesses may be described as *a*, not fearing the spiritual illness, and *b*, fearing the spiritual cure. Further, fear of the spiritual cure may be seen as a kind of fear of spiritual health, that state which results from the spiritual cure.

Kierkegaard goes on to claim that the latter spiritual illness is worse than the former. For it involves a confusion between the punishment and the wrongdoing, that is, between the spiritual cure and the spiritual illness itself. For the man who fears the spiritual cure shows that he sees this, rather than the illness, as the real evil. That is, he takes the cure (punishment) as his illness. Whereas, of course, it is his wrongdoing that is the real illness.

One further claim. The spiritual cure, that is, the punishment for wrongdoing, is a cure only if it is taken by the wrongdoer as punishment, that is, as a cure for his wrongdoing.

These claims bring out very strikingly some important differences between the ideas of spiritual illness and cure and the ordinary ideas of illness and cure. I suppose these differences go to show the force of the idea that such conditions are 'illnesses' and 'cures' regarded *spiritually* — in the words of Kierkegaard.

Ordinarily fear would not be regarded as a kind of 'illness'. So that neither not fearing one's illness nor fearing the medicine would ordinarily be conceived as kinds of further illness. The exception to this is the idea, taken over from psychology into ordinary thought, that there are some conditions of fear, or conditions resembling what we normally conceive as fear, which are pathological. This is the idea that such conditions are forms of psychological illness.

Ordinarily the fear of illness, ill-health or disease, would be regarded as reasonable and proper — 'rational', perhaps. (See my earlier discussion in chapter two.) It would be regarded as a manifestation of mental clarity and balance, as an expression of a reasonable outlook on human existence, on life and death, on activity, and on human needs and capacities.

Ordinarily it would be *not* fearing illness that would be regarded as unreasonable, as evincing a peculiar feature of the judgement (maybe ignorance or lack of proportion), or a peculiar outlook on life. It would be seen as part of a value system which could not, I have argued earlier, be 'reasonable', from the point of view of our natural life on earth.

Ordinarily fear is not seen as a kind of 'illness'. But, even where it can be seen in this way, it is not always or necessarily conceived as an 'illness' of the same category as, or homogeneous with, its object. But the illness identified by Kierkegaard as fear of punishment, like the illness identified as absence of fear of wrongdoing, is homogeneous with its object. Both are spiritual conditions, for example, conditions of the soul, or moral conditions of the subject. However it is quite possible to fear a physical harm or defect.

I want to consider the notion of ethical punishment in the light of these ideas.

The man who wills the Good out of fear of, or for the sake of avoiding, the punishment, may be thinking either of some kind of punishment in this world — a punishment at other people's hands, for example — or of some quite different sort of punishment. The former case involves the idea of heterogeneity as well as the complexities of the latter. So I begin with the latter case, with the idea of there being a kind of 'spiritual' punishment, a kind of punishment one might aptly call ethical, or religious. Kierkegaard calls it the 'punishment of eternity' (p. 82).

Even though the punishment of eternity, whatever this punishment amounts to, is homogeneous with the 'illness' (the wrong-doing), the man who wills the Good out of fear of such punishment is still liable to the accusation that he is double-minded. For, just as with the man who wills the Good for the sake of the reward—whatever he conceives the reward in natural terms or in ethicoreligious terms—and who can be shown to have landed himself in that implicit self-contradiction over intrinsic values which I explored earlier in chapter one, so with the man whose willing of the Good is conditioned by his fear of the punishment. Both are double-minded.

'Double-mindedness' can be understood in at least two distinct ways. One is the idea of heterogeneity of values, the idea that the double-minded man is trying to live at the centre of two incompatible systems of values, typically one this-worldly ('naturalistic') and one other-worldly (for example, religious or ethical). The other is the idea of the conditionality of certain values, in particular the idea that the double-minded man is trying to make his ethical (or religious) life conditional upon its bringing him certain goods. It is the latter aspect that I want to discuss now.

The man who wills the Good out of fear of the 'punishment of eternity'—like the man who wills the Good for the sake of the 'reward of eternity'—is certainly, in both aspects of his mind, considering the idea of 'eternity'. Only it is not necessarily a correct, or adequate, conception of eternity that such a mode of willing exhibits. One point is this. We are supposing that the man who wills the Good out of fear of the punishment of eternity is not making the mistake, if it is one, of thinking of the punishment of eternity as just a punishment in and of and from this world. But it does not follow from his being right in seeing that a distinction has to be made, and right in choosing the alternative of eternity rather than the alternative of this world, that his conception of what eternity's punishment amounts to is also right.

For one might well wonder what conception of the punishment of eternity a man could have, whose conception of *eternity* was that exhibited in his willing the Good out of fear of that punishment.

Willing the Good certainly implies having some conception of eternity, though whether to understand this in ethical or religious terms is not clear. At the very least it is clear that willing the Good implies having some conception of 'the Good'. And this is, I think, all that need be understood by 'eternity'.

So the question to ask is: what conception of the Good does a man show himself to have, who wills the Good out of fear of eternity's punishment, that is, out of fear of some kind of punishment essentially related to, or homogeneous with, the Good or the Good's inmost nature?

I tried to show in chapter one that, if a man purports to will the Good for the sake of the reward—however we understand this reward—he shows himself to have an inadequate, indeed self-contradictory, conception of the ethical. The same proof would suffice here too, since the logical feature of the idea of willing the Good for the sake of the reward upon which rests the inadequacy of the corresponding conception of the Good is reproduced here too.

I think this argument shows, in fact, that such a man cannot have an adequate conception of 'eternity's punishment' either. For his confusion of values, as I tried to disentangle it, reflects a failure to distinguish clearly enough between the ethical and the natural, or, more generally, we might now say, between 'eternity' and its determinations and 'the world' and its determinations.

The success of such an argument rests, obviously, on the assumption of there actually being a sharp distinction between 'eternity' and 'the world'. It rests, in particular, on assuming that there is a sharp distinction between adequate conceptions of eternity and the world in respect of certain logical features of these conceptions; for example, the logical features exhibited in those logical features of thought and speech concerning eternity and the world that I tried to illustrate in chapter one.

According to Kierkegaard, for the man who fails to distinguish between eternity and its determinations and the world and its determinations, the idea of a 'punishment of eternity' cannot *be true* (p. 84). Presumably this implies not just that his idea of eternity's punishment cannot be the right idea, that is, cannot be adequate to the conception properly implied in this description, but also that he must be ignorant, or mistaken, or deluded, or self-deceived about this fact.

I think he could have said also: for such a man the idea of 'eternity' too cannot be true. (For example, he cannot have a correct conception of morality, or religion.) It is only for the man who *truly* wills the Good, as opposed, perhaps *inter alia*, to willing the Good for some reason, that the ideas of the Good, eternity, and eternity's punishment—or reward—can 'be true'.

For the force of the considerations I have been presenting in earlier sections of this work is to drive one to 'see', or believe, that a morality which is identified with nature would simply not count as a 'morality' at all. Now this assumption is obviously arguable, and nearly as obviously impossible to settle decisively by argument.

This observation need not unsettle someone who follows Kierkegaard in using an argument tacitly premised by such an assumption. For, in effect, Kierkegaard goes on to make precisely this observation. But he puts it, characteristically, in his own language. He claims that it is only the man who *truly* wills the Good that is in possession of what might be called a 'proof' for the existence of the Good, that is, the existence of eternity. 'There is only one proof that the Eternal exists: faith in it' (p. 84).

This does not mean that he thinks of truly willing the Good as standing in relation to the Good's existence, or to a proposition asserting the Good's existence, as does the premiss of a valid deductive argument to its conclusion: nor anything like that. Indeed, part of the force of his claim is precisely that no proposition, nor anything else, could possibly have that sort of logical relation to the assertion of the Good's existence. In *that* sense of 'proof', he is quite clear that there can be no 'proof' of the existence of the Good.

One might well query his using the word (concept) 'proof' to describe his idea (see p. 84), in view of this limitation on its sense. Is it not misleading, and can it be anything but misleading, seeing that nothing can be like enough to a 'proof', so understood, to deserve the name of a proof?

I think, nonetheless, there is justification for seeing the matter in terms of the idea of a proof, even if it is granted that this is not exactly the logical, or linguistic, relation normally understood by this word. For I believe it can be shown that there is something available to the man who 'truly wills the Good' which is in an important respect similar to that which must be available to anybody we should ordinarily agree possessed a 'proof' of some proposition.

Informally, one might put the argument as follows. That there *is* such a thing as 'morality', that is, moral responsibility or moral duty or moral value, cannot be 'proved' by any kind of deductive argument. But this does not prevent there being people for whom morality, as described, plays a central part in their outlook on the world. For them there is such a thing as morality. It is impossible to deny that there are people who recognize themselves as subject to moral demands or moral imperatives and even to absolute, unconditional, demands. For such people, we might put it, there is, in their very experience and understanding of the world and life, a kind of 'proof' of morality. Notice, too, that this proof, like a valid deductive argument, expresses the holding of an internal and necessary relation, not a contingent relation.

Obviously—tautologically, perhaps—this sort of proof of the existence of such a thing as morality, so understood, is available *only* to these sorts of people. For someone who does not see life in terms of this idea of morality, moral demands and values, such a proof can be no more than a *fact* about the way someone else looks on things. It would be twice removed from the kind of proof in question. For it would be merely a *fact* about the way things happened to be: nothing necessary. And it would be a fact about some other person's mind, for example, his *understanding or attitudes*: but not about the world, the way things are.

It would follow, if this line of thought is correct, that a man who does not see 'eternity' in the kind of way indicated cannot be said to have any sort of proof whatever for the existence of eternity. That is to say, that *even from his own point of view*, the assumption that there is such a thing as eternity (the absolute moral demand) must forever necessarily remain a mere unfounded and unfoundable assumption.

Worse. For it seems to me to be implied, in the line of argument I used earlier (p. 74), that for such a man the 'assumption' that there is such a thing as eternity cannot make any coherent sense.

If this is so, the notion of 'double-mindedness' has to be taken in a very strong sense indeed. For it is implied, I think, that such a man, in speaking and 'thinking' in terms of eternity and its characteristic rewards and punishments, is using ideas which can have no sense for him. And it is hard to understand such a condition, except in terms of the idea of self-deceit.

Let us return to the idea of a man's purportedly willing the Good out of fear of the punishment. There is a second point of strangeness about this idea.

I have argued that such a man cannot be seen as having a true, correct, understanding of the Good, 'eternity'. Now someone who fears to do wrong because of the punishment shows that he fears the punishment. We are here considering only the idea of 'eternity's punishment'. This is, whatever it is, distinct from any sort of 'punishment' issued in and by the world; that is, any sort of natural harm—whether this comes in the form of punishments inflicted by civil or religious authorities, or by one's parents, or in the form of disease, harm, or misfortune. Either can be seen, I think, as 'punishment for wrongdoing'. But the idea of eternity's punishment should be distinguished from an idea of natural harm.

This needs clarification. For certainly someone who looks on the natural, and 'chance', misfortunes of his life as punishments for his wrongdoings does not see these misfortunes as punishments arranged by and inflicted by human authorities. He is clear about this! In that case, there seem to be two possible views he may take on the relation between his wrongdoing and this 'punishment'

He may see these natural misfortunes as inflicted upon him not by human authorities, nor by chance, but by something like the divine will—as a punishment inflicted by God. Presumably God could, if he had wished, have operated through human authorities, so that such a man would regard the punishments inflicted upon him by merely human authorities as divine punishments too.

To look on the relation thus is to conceive of God (the divine) as 'rewarding' and 'punishing' good or evil behaviour by natural goods and evils, for example, by wealth or poverty. And this is, once again, to make the mistake of confusing moral and natural goods—the mistake over the logic of 'rewards' and 'punishments' —that I discussed earlier under the rubric of 'homogeneity' in chapter one.

For such a man there is no essential difference between the world's punishments and the punishments of eternity. Admittedly, the former come from the world, the latter come from the divine will. But both operate within the world in the form of natural evils, or natural harm. For such a man, what makes some event in which he is concerned a 'punishment' is the same irrespective of whether he conceived the punishment as one of the world or one of eternity. It is a punishment simply because it involves his suffering the infliction of *natural* evils.

The alternative view such a man might take of the relation between wrongdoing and the 'punishment of eternity' is this. He might conceive of some kind of natural relation, perhaps mechanical, perhaps causal, perhaps both. The oddity about this conception appears to be the latent idea that a natural relation can hold between terms which are not themselves natural.

Of course the 'punishment' is a natural occurrence, describable, we may suppose, in natural terms, for example, in terms of some natural sciences. But the 'wrongdoing' is not. The man's doing wrong is, of course, his actually doing something, and this act is quite properly conceived as a 'natural' occurrence. But this aspect of his activity is not all there is to its being an instance of wrongdoing. (This is a familiar enough point.)

A natural relation, for example, a causal one, can quite well be conceived to hold between that *natural* event which is (but is not identical with) his wrongdoing, and the natural event which he identifies as a punishment for his wrongdoing. (I say 'quite well', but obviously a man who genuinely believed in the existence of such relations would be held insane or superstitious.) But here too it is not clear what justifies the claim that the existence of such a relation would be sufficient to make the natural occurrence which befalls the wrongdoer eternity's punishment—or any sort of punishment, indeed—for his wrongdoing.

It is not that he argues from the existence of such relations between his wrongdoing and subsequent occurrences *to* the notion that these occurrences are eternity's punishment for his wrongdoing. Rather, he argues *from* his recognition of some such occurrence as eternity's punishment for his wrongdoing *to* the notion that there must be some natural relation between these two 'occurrences'. Though even here he is confused, as I argued.

So what his idea of 'eternity's punishment' is remains quite confused. For it is not simply the idea of a natural evil that is the (natural) consequence of his wrongdoing. Not every such evil consequence need be regarded by him as a punishment. Rather, he recognizes some such 'consequences' as punishments in advance of perceiving the relation which makes these events natural consequences of his wrongdoing.

There must, then, apparently, be some other criterion which enables him to identify some natural evils as 'punishments', and therefore as natural consequences, of his wrongdoing. There must be some quality peculiar to just these occurrences in his life. But his position does not seem to allow for the possibility of there being any such further criterion.

Let us return to the point that to will the Good out of fear of 'eternity's punishment' implies, very obviously, fearing this punishment. But we have now established that this cannot possibly amount to fearing some natural evil or other, for no natural evil can coherently be seen as eternity's punishment.

Eternity's punishment must be some kind of 'evil', or 'harm', which is homogeneous with the nature of 'eternity'. This is as yet puzzling. It might mean some kind of 'ethical evil' or 'ethical harm', or some kind of 'religious harm'. But what these phrases might mean is also puzzling.

Nonetheless, we need not, I think, understand exactly what is meant in order to realize that such a man's mind must contain at least a serious confusion, and perhaps a self-contradiction.

For fearing the punishment of eternity must be fearing something—apparently some evil of some kind—that is conceived as *essentially* connected with 'eternity', with the divine will. For example, fearing the wrath of God is obviously fearing something that is essentially connected with God, with his being and nature. And one might put this as follows. Fearing eternity's punishment must be fearing some essential aspect, or essential property, of eternity. And this amounts to fearing something that is essential to eternity's being 'eternity'. The man who fears (in the manner under discussion) the wrath of God, can be described also as *fearing God*.

This is the strangeness in such a man's conception of 'the Good'. One might put it thus: he claims, or appears to recognize, that there is such a thing as 'the Good', and this claim is apparently borne out in his 'willing the Good'. But he also appears to *fear* something that can be seen to be an essential part, or aspect, of the Good, namely, its peculiar punishment. And to fear some aspect of the Good implies seeing that aspect of the Good as *undesirable*, as an *evil* of some kind.

Thus his conception is implicitly self-contradictory, insofar as it can be understood at all. He has, or purports to have, some conception of the Good that is partly a conception of something evil.

I want to repeat, in a somewhat altered form, some of this argument. This will bring out another misconception that may be ascribed to a man who purports to will the Good for the sake of avoiding the punishment, and, correspondingly, another feature of the logic of Kierkegaard's concept of 'the Good'.

Someone who purports to will the Good for the sake of avoiding the punishment has two ideas at once before his mind: the idea of the Good and the idea of punishment. Now there are two possible attitudes one can have towards the relation between these ideas. One can hold either that the relation is external and accidental or that it is internal and essential. To hold the latter is, implicitly, to hold that there is really only one entity in question: the Good together with its punishment. To hold the former is to hold that there are really two distinct entities (occurrences), and thus, implicitly, that one might exist without the other. So such a man is committed, it appears, to holding that it is possible that the Good might exist without the punishment.

Now there is an obvious sense in which the latter is possible. For it is possible that the Good might exist, although no *natural* punishment should follow wrongdoing.

One must be careful, in extending this possibility, not to allow it to appear, contrary to what has been said before, that a man might coherently suppose that there was such a thing as the Good and, at the same time, think of these natural evils as punishments for wrongdoing, that is, for failure to will the Good. This has already been shown to be confused. What we are supposing is that someone holds that the Good might exist, even though nothing like a 'punishment from the Good'—eternity's punishment— existed.

Precisely analogously, we might suppose that someone believed that there was such a thing as the Good, but not such a thing as the reward of the Good.

At this point, perhaps, the thrust of the arguments changes direction somewhat. Previously it has been directed mainly against certain false conceptions of what a 'reward for willing the Good' or a 'punishment for not willing the Good' might be, involving correspondingly false, or confused, conceptions of the Good. And this might lead a hasty reader to suppose that the main, and so far hidden, thrust has been against *all* conceptions of a reward or punishment appropriate to the Good.

This is not so. For Kierkegaard will now begin to expose some of the true implications, some of the genuine features, of these concepts. And now the thrust of the arguments is against the idea that the Good might have nothing like a 'reward' associated with it.

If Kierkegaard holds that a man who purports to will the Good out of fear of the punishment thereby shows himself to have a conception of the Good such that the Good might conceivably exist without the punishment, and if he also holds that the latter idea is false or incoherent (I believe the latter), then he must himself believe at least *either* that such a man has tried to make an impossible connection between 'willing the Good' and 'fearing the punishment', *or* that there is some mistake or incoherency in the very idea he shows himself to have of 'fearing the punishment'.

My view is that Kierkegaard believes both. He believes, for reasons already given, that it is incoherent to relate the idea of fearing the punishment to the idea of willing the Good as *reason*, or *motive*, for willing the Good. And he believes, congruently with this, that in the ordinary sense there is an incoherency in the idea that a man who wills the Good might also *fear* the punishment. It is this second belief that I am now beginning to explore.

Kierkegaard holds that someone who, explicitly or implicitly, believes that the Good might exist even though nothing like a 'punishment' (or 'reward') existed must be wrong, and even incoherent in his beliefs. For the *punishment is part of the Good*, or the reward is part of the Good. Not only is the punishment, like the reward, properly regarded as part of the Good—as entailed in the very conception of the Good—but also it is properly to be regarded as a help, and aid, in willing the Good.

Now the man who claims to will the Good for the sake of avoiding the punishment—or for the sake of gaining the reward —has seen this point, only he has seen it dimly and confusedly. For what is implied by this view is that the punishment, that is, the true punishment, is to be regarded as something desirable. It is, in fact, not an evil at all, regarded from the point of view of 'the Good' or eternity, for example, from the moral point of view. Rather, it is a good.

One might exemplify this claim by saying that the idea of an ethical punishment, for example, is the idea of something which, from the ethical point of view, is necessarily seen as an ethical good, and not an ethical evil.

Implicit, again, is the idea that the ethical punishment must be seen not as a kind of ethical harm, but rather as the opposite: a kind of ethical medicine or cure and something that does the subject good, from the ethical point of view. This idea can mean only that the subject is made ethically better. However, this does not imply the probably false claim that the punishment must always appear as nothing but a good. For one thing, one's ethical vision, one's ethical capacities and position, may not be up to this exalted level. For another, there must necessarily be always a sense in which the punishment is an evil, even ethically speaking, to the subject, however ethically exalted his outlook. Otherwise it simply would not make sense to call it, or see it as, a 'punishment', even ethically speaking.

What is difficult is to reconcile the claims *a*, that the notion of the ethical punishment, if properly explained, is the notion of something that is ethically regarded a *good*, and *b*, that the notion of ethical punishment is necessarily also the notion of something that is, even ethically regarded, an *evil*. What is difficult is to explain how these two claims can be referred to different aspects of the punishment.

I defer this question to chapter four for more discussion, in order to briefly consider here the third point arising out of the idea of a man's willing the Good for the sake of avoiding the punishment, understanding this in the sense of the punishment of eternity.

Implicit in such a man's mind must be two ideas about the way to the Good. Explicit, at least, is the idea that the Good (the good will) can be reached by way of a kind of willing motivated by the very fear of punishment he emphasizes. Implicit, one may suppose, is the idea that the Good may be reached by a kind of direct willing, that is, an act of will that is not motivated by a fear of punishment or desire of reward, but simply, perhaps, by a love or desire of the Good for its own sake.

That this idea is implicit must follow from his wishing to conceive the Good as something which is intrinsically good, as something desirable in and for itself—what other sense could the notion have? For it follows from this that there is at least the possibility of its being desired for itself, and from this the possibility of its being willed for itself. This does not seem, perhaps, a very strange idea. For it is based on an obvious and obviously acceptable truth about ways and means; namely, that on earth if one wants to get to a certain place, there is in practice almost always, and in theory necessarily always, a number of different routes one can take.

We should notice, though, that the force of this truism is immediately weakened even when we transfer it analogically merely as far as the realm of the psychological, or epistemological. It is by no means so obvious, given any psychological condition, for example, a state of the passions or of knowledge, that there can always be in principle a number of different routes to achieving this condition. For example, it is not at all obvious that there are different ways to achieve one and the same scientific, or philosophical, skill. Even here, it begins to look as if the 'way' one sets out upon the travels has a decisive influence upon the possible destinations at which one may arrive.

Latent in the idea that any given 'place' may always, and

necessarily so, be reached by a number of different 'paths' is the idea that the concept of the place and the concept of the path are distinct, and the idea that the place and the path are external to each other in a certain sense.

Kierkegaard claims quite sharply that, 'spiritually' considered, the ideas of 'place' and 'path' lose just that feature which is brought out in the truism I mentioned.

In matters of religion and morality, as much as, say, education, we are concerned, among other things, with the state of the subject's soul, or his character—however exactly one identifies it. At any rate, religion and ethics deal with what is ordinarily thought to be some 'inward' characteristics of the subject, that is, just those characteristics that constitute him as a 'subject' and as the 'subject' he identifiably is.

Kierkegaard identifies the spiritual analogue of 'place' with the idea of the *state* of the soul, and the spiritual analogue of 'path' with the idea of the *changing* of the soul (pp. 84, 85). And these identifications can easily be made, in only slightly altered terms, for a purely ethical conception of the human being.

The place, then, is regarded as a state of the human individual, religiously or ethically speaking. And the path is regarded as the changing in this state; one might say: the path is the change from one ethical condition to another, for example, ethical improvement or degeneration, generally speaking.

The phrase 'willing the Good' might be understood to mean either the ultimately desired state of the individual, or that transitory and changing series of conditions which leads towards such a state. (I do not think that Kierkegaard believed this distinction could be made out sharply.)

'Fearing the punishment' must, on the face of it, mean some different or separable state of the mind or soul. If this is so, the man described as willing the Good out of fear of the punishment is being credited with these two distinguishable conditions, and a certain connection is being implied to hold between them. We are asked to suppose that he is, so to speak, spiritually travelling towards the state of 'willing the Good' by the path of 'fearing the punishment'.

Now I believe Kierkegaard's point is that fearing the punishment is the wrong path—a path which could never possibly lead to such a state, that is, to 'the Good', or eternity. It is not that there is no path. There is indeed a path towards the Good, but it is describable as 'willing the Good', which cannot be distinguished from the 'state' it is conceived as leading towards.

I want now to consider an example, a notion, which is certainly implied in Kierkegaard's discussion of 'willing the Good out of fear of punishment'; this may help to throw light on some of the obscurities in the claims he makes about this idea. I want to consider some logical, and ethical, features of the notion of a man's purporting to 'do his duty out of fear of punishment'.

One can say at once of such a man that, in thinking of his duty, he has two quite different things in his mind. He has in mind the idea of his duty, whatever it amounts to, as 'duty'. And he has in mind the idea that if he fails to do his duty, he is liable to punishment. Further, this latter idea is operative as his motive, or reason, for doing his duty.

But not only this. For one might well ask what his conceiving of his duty as 'duty' can imply, if it does not, at least, imply therein a sufficient motive for doing his duty, whatever this duty is. It implies what we may call a 'moral motive', a 'moral reason'. Seeing his duty as 'duty' does not, of course, specify the action, nor the reasons that might be given for performing it, in any detail. It merely indicates that he sees it as an action for which there is some sufficient moral reason.

Now fear of punishment may very well operate as a motive for action in a man's mind. Nothing is more naturally intelligible. Only it cannot, from a certain point of view, be understood as operating as a moral motive—a 'moral incentive'—for action.

We might reason as follows. Certainly a man can act out of fear of punishment. And certainly, as implied, fear of punishment can be his *only* motive for action.

But, if he sees the action in question as his 'duty', implicit already in the way he sees the action, the description which he gives to his action, is the belief that he has sufficient reason for doing it. And the further belief that this reason is necessarily a moral reason. It is implied in the description 'doing his duty out of fear of punishment' that the man's *sole* motive for doing his duty was his fear of punishment. That is, it is implied that no other motive than this was operative in his doing his duty. It follows that it is implied that the moral motive, implicit in the very recognition of his duty as 'duty', cannot have been operative in his doing his duty. It is still possible, of course, that he recognized the act in question to be his duty. But it is impossible that this recognition played any part in bringing about his doing his duty.

'Out of fear of punishment' is ambiguous. It might simply mean that his fear of punishment was the cause of his action. But if this is the meaning, it is hard to understand how his action can be judged in moral terms at all, since part of the force of saying that it was caused by his fear is that his fear was sufficient to bring it about that he acted as he did. It does not seem, for familiar reasons, that such an action could properly be judged to have been freely chosen or intentionally performed, in the sense that would justify our judging it in moral terms.

'Out of fear', on the other hand, might mean that his fear of punishment, that is, his recognition of the likelihood of unpleasant consequences for failure, was the reason for which he performed the action. This would assimilate the explanation implicit in our description to a means–end explanation of action. It would imply, I think, that avoidance of these unpleasant consequences functioned in the man's deliberation as the 'end', to be achieved by performance of the action identified as his 'duty'. Here, too, the idea that the action was his duty is implied to have been quite inoperative in his thinking.

Now there is one important difference between the example of 'doing one's duty out of fear of punishment' and 'willing the Good out of fear of punishment'. The former purports to describe an *action*, together with its motive. But the latter does not describe what would ordinarily be called an action, though 'willing the Good' may certainly name something that is present in and behind some actions, for example, the motive or reason the agent has for doing them.

The recognition of the action in question as his duty might be quite inoperative in the man's mind for at least two reasons. One is that the man is of the type sometimes conceived as 'weak-willed'. Whatever this means positively, it means, negatively, at least that the man's full and clear recognition of his duty may not be sufficient to motivate him to do his duty.

This description has a possible application to the case under discussion. It is possible that our man is simply weak-willed, and that this is the reason why it is his fear of punishment, rather than his recognition of the act as his duty, that is *operative* in his practical thinking.

But this cannot possibly fit the Kierkegaardian idea of 'willing the Good out of fear of punishment'. 'Weakness of will' could not possibly be given as the explanation for *this* performance.

But if weakness of will is ruled out as an explanation for the failure of the man's recognition of his duty to motivate him, it seems the only other possible explanation is that, in some sense, he has failed to recognize quite fully and clearly that the action in question is his 'duty'.

CHAPTER 4　The idea of
justice
in morality

N ow and then someone speaks of "suffering punishment; when one does the Good". How is that possible? From whom shall that punishment come?' (*Purity of Heart,* p. 97). Kierkegaard proceeds to argue that the idea of 'suffering punishment when one does the Good' is incoherent. And I shall follow his arguments and try to bring out what is implied in them.

Consider who is supposed to be punishing the one who does the Good—who does his duty or acts righteously. Could it be God, the divine source of all goodness? Obviously not, on almost any familiar understanding of this concept. Without wanting to offer anything as restricting as a definition, we might say that the concepts 'God', 'the Good' or 'goodness', and 'reward' are closely interconnected. God is the rewarder of goodness. Goodness is what is rewarded by God. What God gives for goodness is the reward.

There is a related view that goodness is its own reward. Then again it would be nonsensical to claim that a man could be 'punished' for doing the Good. For in the light of this view 'punishment' is simply the correlative of wrongdoing. Wrongdoing is its own punishment. But there is something right about this last view, and what that is will, I hope, emerge in a later discussion in this chapter.

Then could it be 'the world' that punishes the doing of good? Could it be the earthly, human authorities with which the law makes us familiar, or which structure our family and professional lives? Could it, perhaps, be the blind forces of nature? (Notice that all of these can be, and have been, conceived as providing us with the punishments for our wrongdoing, for example, as agents, perhaps unconscious, of the divine will.) But this supposition too is impossible. And it can be claimed to be impossible, I think, because of part of the logic of the concepts. For one can claim that it is part of the concept of punishment that only if a man is guilty can he be punished. There may be other conditions too. For example, he can be punished only for that offence of which he is guilty.

To hold this view would not necessarily be to hold the view, obviously false, that even an innocent man cannot be harmed, and even harmed for that very deed or mode of activity which, although taken as the grounds for the harm inflicted on him, in fact constitutes his innocence. Nor would it necessarily be to hold the view, equally obviously false, that such harm cannot be inflicted with the idea that it is genuine punishment. Those who inflict such harm upon an innocent man may well believe that in so harming, or even killing, him they are punishing him. For they may well believe him to be guilty, or even conceive of what actually constitutes his innocence as constituting some form of offence.

In reply to this argument it may be said that such things can easily happen as just described. It simply needs to be added that, in such cases, the punishment inflicted is unjust. This reply is certainly simple and clear, but I do not think it has the overwhelming power it may seem to have. It may, in turn, be answered that such a reply rests on a conceptual confusion.

For it might, I believe, be argued that the concept of punishment is, at least, the concept of some harm or evil which is given in *just* recompense for guilt, that the concept of punishment already involves the concept of justice in some such way. If this view is justified, it will follow that the description 'unjust punishment' must contain a latent self-contradiction. For it will amount to the description of something purported to be given in both just and unjust recompense. To argue thus is not, of course, to deny that we can mistakenly believe an innocent man to deserve punishment, that is, to believe that he can be punished.

I do not want to claim this view—this counterargument—for my own, nor do I want to claim that it fits easily with ordinary conceptions of punishment, whatever precisely these may be. For I do not intend to deny that we do ordinarily, and quite intelligibly, speak of 'just' and 'unjust' punishment! And if the view I sketched were correct, such locutions would be either self-contradictory or redundant.

But I do want to claim that this view partly expresses a particular ethical outlook, or, perhaps, a family of related outlooks; and that it is not, taken on its own terms, internally incoherent—except perhaps for a point I shall bring up at the end of this chapter. And I want also to claim that it is an outlook that seems to have been sincerely and consciously held, even by some intelligent people. Kierkegaard, indeed, was one of them. Maybe the Plato of the *Gorgias* was another. Simone Weil was perhaps a third. I want to claim that the moral philosopher has at the very least a duty to accept this curious belief as one of the 'phenomena'.

Suppose we did not accept the counterargument I sketched above, but rested content with the familiar idea which it counters. Suppose we assume, for the time being, that such harm as 'the world' mistakenly visits upon an innocent man is to be counted as the world's 'punishment' of that man. (Remember that I am not discussing the punishment of legal, or political, or social offences, but only the punishment of 'moral offences', for example, of moral wrongdoings.) This is, at the very least, to suppose that the harm so inflicted can in logic count as a punishment for a moral wrongdoing (or an alleged moral wrongdoing).

Now, whatever exactly the idea of justice is, we cannot, I think, avoid assuming that it must still even here characterize the relation between the punishment and the offence. Even in the world's eyes its punishments are still to be counted as just or, in unhappy instances, unjust. But to make this minimal assumption commits us to another assumption. It commits us to assuming that justice and injustice can characterize the relation between a *natural* event, that is, the event which consists in the infliction of that harm upon the offender that is here being conceived as his punishment, and an *ethical* event—if this phrase makes sense—namely, the evil (or good) deed for which this punishment is being inflicted. This may look like a small and trivial assumption. But, in the eyes of someone who adheres to the view of morality I sketched in chapter two, it is far likelier to appear a huge and monstrous confusion that vitiates the whole of this familiar ethical outlook.

What is at stake in this conflict is not just a logical point about the concept of punishment, for example, the question whether or not it is a necessary truth that only the guilty can be punished. What is at stake here is the concept of *justice*, or more precisely, *ethical justice*.

It is a conflict which undercuts the earlier conflict I touched upon. *Now* it is not just a question of whether or not it makes sense to conceive of an 'unjust punishment'. It is, rather, the much wider and quite distinct question of the nature of the relationship that is implied between action and consequences when we speak of the 'justice' or 'injustice' of punishment—or reward.

Let us make clear exactly what this present objection comes to.

In the field of the merely legal we may suppose both parties to the conflict are in fundamental agreement. They both agree that it makes sense to think of justice and injustice as implying relations between those deeds which count in the legal system as punishable offences and those events which count there as their punishments.

What allows the 'transcendentalist' (for such in essence he is) to agree with the ordinary man about this legal justice is that he can perfectly well see both crime and punishment as commensurable, since both are *phenomena*. (Of course, more can be said on this point.) If one raises the tricky question of *mens rea*, or intention, the transcendentalist need not be disturbed. These too, he can claim, are established by 'phenomenal' means, such as scientific and inductive, and may therefore themselves be regarded as mere denizens of the phenomenal world too. But what the transcendentalist claims, with respect to the ethical, is that since the relations of justice and injustice presuppose some kind of *commensurability* of values, and since there is no commensurability of values, in the required sense, between the *ethical* evil of wrongdoing and the merely *natural* evil of the harm whose infliction is the punishment for this wrongdoing, it follows that no relation between these two values could be characterized either as just or as unjust. And from this, again, it follows that it cannot be possible to regard the natural evil in question as the punishment for the wrongdoing.

If justice means anything special when we are speaking ethically —as contrasted with, say, the legal, political, or social realms— it means, on this view, that there must at least be an *essential* relationship between the deed and the consequence. That is to say, the reward or punishment must be a good or evil of the same category as is the deed.

This implies that if the deed to be rewarded or punished is seen in its ethical aspects—if the kind of reward and punishment involved is 'ethical' reward or punishment—then the goods or evils which are given to the agent as reward or punishment for his deed must themselves be ethical goods or ethical evils.

The relation of ethical justice, which links the ethical deed and the ethical outcome that is its punishment, cannot be simply a contingent and accidental relation. It must be a necessary relation between the ethical deed and ethical outcome. In other words, the idea that some punishment was the *just* outcome of a man's wrongdoing cannot be the idea that some proposition is *contingently* true. The relation of ethical justice, one might put it, is an internal relation—however this term may be defined.

However, the connection between the action, which seen as an instance of wrongdoing is seen as requiring punishment, and the event which is seen as constituting its punishment, cannot be more than a contingent, perhaps causal, connection. And generally we may assume that no two phenomena—no two events in the world—can be related other than contingently, externally, and accidentally.

This assumption would be sufficient to prove at least that no natural event could possibly count as the 'ethical punishment' for a misdeed. And this holds, whatever view is taken of the ontological status of the latter ethical deed.

But the requirement of an internal and necessary relation implies more than the requirement that the 'ethical punishment' of a deed should not be identified with any *event* that is the outcome of that deed. For if the deed itself is regarded simply as a natural event, we shall be committed to the idea that a necessary and internal relation might hold between two terms, one of which (the punishment) is *not* a natural event (phenomenon), but rather some kind of ethical outcome, the other of which *is* no more than a natural event. To suppose this possible is, implicitly, to suppose it possible that there might be an internal and necessary relation between terms of different ontological categories. And this is impossible.

It is from this that the demand for 'commensurability' of values flows in part. For the demand that the relation of ethical justice should be an internal relation implies a demand that the 'values' between which such a relation holds should themselves be *homogeneous*.

If this is justified, it will at once follow that the idea that 'the good' could be 'punished' contains a latent self-contradiction. For it follows that there can be no such internal relation between doing good and that evil in which the punishment is thought to consist as is necessary. And this is true irrespective of whether that evil is conceived as natural or ethical.

Let us return to the very first ideas I broached, the idea that it is quite senseless to suppose God, or the Good, might 'punish' the doing of good. Why is this senseless? Obviously because the idea of 'punishment' is the idea of some *evil*, and maybe some harm, inflicted for the doing of something itself seen as some kind of evil, whether ethical or not.

Neither party in the dispute I have so far talked about wishes to deny that punishment is necessarily some kind of evil. They do disagree about the ontological category of evil that the specific idea of 'ethical' punishment can represent. For the ordinary man, the natural evils visited upon the wrongdoer by society or its legal institutions can count as the punishment for a purely ethical wrong. For the transcendentalist, only an 'ethical evil'—whatever exactly this idea comes to—can count as the punishment for an 'ethical wrong'.

This distinction has to be carried through. For it allows the transcendentalist to claim, quite consistently in his logic, that even natural *goods* may be, ethically speaking, evil. And conversely, even natural evils may be, ethically speaking, good.

This way of putting the matter is seriously loose, but some examples will help clarify the point. A wrongdoer whose wrongdoing is succeeded not by, say, ignominy and imprisonment, but by wealth and honour will, of course, be universally agreed to have received what are in natural terms good things. But this does not, for the transcendentalist, entail that he has received anything like an 'ethical reward'. Indeed, he may go so far as to claim that the very natural goodness of these 'rewards' (apparent rewards) constitutes one respect in which from the ethical point of view they are evils for the wrongdoer. That is, what looks like a reward from the world's point of view may, partly for that reason, be from the ethical point of view a punishment.

Conversely, the Christian martyred for his faith will be universally acknowledged to have suffered a great natural evil —what greater than a martyr's death? But of course this does not imply that he has suffered (whatever this sense of suffering is) an ethical, or religious, evil. On the contrary. It can be claimed that such a death is the crown and reward of his life of faith.

It is important not to confuse the justification of this way of looking at good and evil things with any specifically religious or theological dogma. For instance, it does not rest on belief in a personal immortality, with or without belief in a 'personal' God who judges us after death. It is a way of looking at these matters which can characterize a man who is quite irreligious, quite atheistic, in such terms. In traditional ethical terminology, it may characterize the man who sees morality from a 'deontological' point of view, and a very strictly carried through version of this too.

I believe, as a matter of fact, that it is not even sufficient to be religious for the ascription of such an ethical outlook as I have been describing to make sense. For one's conception of the goods of religion, for example, the rewards of the afterlife, may still lay one open to the charge that one's conception of the relation between the good life and its eternal rewards is the conception of a relation of heterogeneity. (What have golden pavements and black-eyed houris to do with the moral virtues?)

The idea of an 'ethical evil' or 'ethical good', as it occurs in the ethical outlook I have been trying to describe, is admittedly very obscure and difficult to grasp. It may have still greater logical defects: this remains to be seen.

I said that the transcendentalist has no wish to deny that the idea of a punishment is necessarily the idea of some kind of evil. For him, the idea of an ethical punishment, in particular, is the idea of some 'ethical evil', and it is the latter idea that needs explanation. For he has no wish to deny, in the second place, that there can be, or may be, such things as ethical evils, and that there can be such things as ethical punishments, that is, events which must be construed from an ethical point of view as punishment.

But 'ethical justice', whatever exactly it means, is obviously thought of as some kind of *good*, and, further, some kind of *ethical* good. Thus, from the ethical point of view, justice is certainly something to be desired. It follows from this general principle that the ethical wrongdoer, so far as he still retains the ethical point of view as so identified, must desire justice. But, since justice in his case amounts to the infliction of, and the suffering of, an ethical punishment for his wrongdoing, the wrongdoer must desire his own ethical punishment.

There is an apparent paradox in this claim, and it is important to be as clear as possible about the respective components of the claim, in order to be clear about the nature and status of this paradox.

The paradox may be put in at least two ways. It might be said that such a man has to see his punishment as both an ethical good and an ethical evil, and that the genus of the 'ethical' does not make so much difference to the generic concepts of good and evil as to prevent the special concepts 'ethical good' and 'ethical evil' from being mutually exclusive. Or it might be said that he must both desire and fear the punishment: desire both its presence and its absence. And that any such pair of conditions can be present only in a mind in which there is a radical division of the will.

One might reply that there are (at least) two quite different senses of 'fear'. In one sense, perhaps the more usual, fearing something implies thinking of it as somehow an evil. The other does not carry this implication. For instance, when we speak of the 'fear of God', we obviously do not wish to imply that since God is rightly to be feared there must be something morally 'evil' to Him.

There is an answer. It can be said that God is rightly to be feared, for there is in Him something that is very definitely an 'evil' to the natural man and in the natural man's terms. In other words, the kind of fear which it is right and proper for a man to feel before God — before the idea of God — is the kind of fear appropriate to the natural man and his conceptions. We might call this 'natural fear'.

Natural fear may be opposed to 'ethical fear', and we may go on to claim that it is precisely ethical fear that it is wrong to feel before God, or the Good, the idea of goodness, or the idea of virtue. Since natural and ethical fear are thus contrasted, there is no contradiction whatever in supposing that a man might feel natural fear before God, but at the same time feel a kind of ethical hope or desire. *Qua* natural man, he should fear God; *qua* ethical subject, he should trust in God and hope for salvation.

So it is not that there is any sense of fear that fails to carry the implication of evil. Each sense of fear carries such an implication. Only each sense carries the appropriate implication. Ethical fear implies the idea of an ethical evil; natural fear implies the idea of a natural evil. So ethical fear is consistent with the idea of the thing feared as, naturally conceived, a good. And natural fear is consistent with the idea of the thing as, ethically seen, good.

This distinction will, I think, dissolve the apparent paradox. For it allows us, certainly, to say that ethical punishment should be feared ethically, but not necessarily naturally. But we also have to say that the relation of ethical justice should be desired and welcomed *ethically*. It is thus not that there is an ethical fear together with a natural desire or hope in such a man's mind. There is an ethical fear and ethical desire, and the paradox remains, though perhaps in a sharper form.

I have said that the idea of ethical justice is obviously the idea of some kind of ethical good. But not what kind of ethical good, if, that is, we may speak of different kinds of ethical good. Perhaps I should say: what is so far not clear is what makes ethical justice an ethical good. For what reasons is it such a good? Clearing this matter up may throw light on the paradox.

Both the wrongdoing and its punishment are ethical evils. So one might think that the relation of justice between the two is simply their 'sum', so to speak: justice equals wrongdoing *plus* punishment. But to say this would be to say that an ethical good (justice) could simply be the 'sum' of two ethical evils.

I do not think such a view has to be rejected immediately as nonsense. For the 'natural' analogue of illness and medicine yields a conclusion which is not necessarily nonsense at all. It can be said that the illness and its appropriate cure are both, naturally speaking, evils, for example, painful. But certainly, given the illness, it is better, naturally speaking, that the patient should suffer the cure rather than not suffer it. For only by suffering the cure will he be cured, that is, relieved of the initial evil of his illness. So it seems to follow that the illness *plus* the medicine is 'better', in some sense, than the illness without the medicine — or, surely, better than the medicine without the illness! And this is to say: two natural evils are better than one!

This analogy does not, of course, show even in its own proper sphere that two natural evils can amount to a natural *good*. But it does seem to show that it makes sense to think of the second evil, when superadded to the first, as producing a state of affairs which is *better* than the mere obtaining of the first. So, arithmetically speaking, the addition of this second evil certainly seems to function as the addition of a good.

The analogy breaks down, among other things, at the point at which the nature of the relationship—the reason for this peculiarity of values—comes into play. In the latter case the relation is a causal and contingent one. It is because giving the sufferer the medicine *brings about* the disappearance of the initial state of illness and the appearance of a state of health, that is, brings about the replacing of a natural evil by a natural good, that we can think of the matter in the way outlined above. Because of this any apparent paradox in the matter vanishes on inspection. For we are here dealing with a temporal succession of different natural conditions, the earliest being evil, the latest, hopefully, good.

It is not that there is no question of temporal succession in the ethical case. For it makes sense to see part of the ethical function of punishment as the bringing about of some kind of restoration of the (ethical) status quo, that is, as the bringing about of some kind of ethically desirable condition out of an initial ethically undesirable condition. This is, I suppose, a common view of the function of punishment. And therefore, indirectly, of justice.

But this view is inadequate. For ethical justice can be seen as something that is, ethically speaking, a good in and for itself: thus, it can be seen as a good regardless of whether it is the function of bringing about a change for the better in the ethical situation. (Repulsive as it seems, this assertion can be given as the form of a Christian justification for hell, the 'punishment of eternity'.) And it is how an ethical good of this sort can be 'constituted' by two ethical evils that remains puzzling and paradoxical.

One might escape from the difficulty by identifying ethical justice with the relationship of homogeneity of (ethical) value between the wrongdoing and its punishment. Since this does not seem to allow for the dimension of 'weight' of ethical values, we shall have to identify ethical justice, specifically, with the relationship of *identity* of ethical values. In more traditional terms, we may identify ethical justice with the relation of 'balance', recompense, or restitution that has often been conceived to characterize punishment.

This identification is not enough to solve the problem, for it demands a further presumption. It is necessary that this relation — whatever exactly is meant by 'recompense' in the ethical sphere — should itself be conceived as an ethical good, and moreover a good in itself.

This is, I think, a possible position, in that it does not seem necessarily self-contradictory, nor yet insane, and has, perhaps, been held by several thinkers in the past. But it is not very satisfactory, since it appears to most people to reduce the idea of ethical justice to an idea which is both narrower and more formal than that idea. I think, for most people, the idea of ethical justice implies or includes the idea of recompense, and that indeed this recompense may be seen as the 'formal' component of the idea of ethical justice, but without exhausting this idea. And, finally, I doubt if this is Kierkegaard's own understanding of the idea.

For it is possible to make an important distinction of conceptions here. On one hand, it might be held that what is, ethically speaking, good in itself is the conjunction or totality of the wrongdoing and its punishment. This is the first view I indicated above. Next, it might be held that what is ethically good in itself is the relation between the wrongdoing and the punishment, for example, a relation of recompense or identity. What is good is that the punishment stand ethically to the wrongdoing as its recompense, its ethical 'equivalent'. This is, roughly, the view indicated just above. But, quite differently from either of these, it might be held that what is good in itself is the punishment the occurrence of which constitutes the punishment—if, and only if, it falls upon a wrongdoer.

It is easy to miss this third possibility. For it has the form of a claim that *if* the wrongdoing occurs, then the punishment is a good in itself. And it is easy to think that this claim is self-contradictory and merely a confused way of making one of the two former claims sketched just above. But this is not so. It is, I think, a perfectly consistent and viable position to hold.

There is a further possible objection to the second of these views, the view that while wrongdoing and punishment are both evils, justice, as the ethical relation between them, is a good. It may be said that this claim has a specious air of sense about it. And that this vanishes if we distinguish as sharply as we may between the idea of an ethical relation such as justice and the idea of a natural relation.

A 'natural relation', one might claim, is a relation between two natural, objective, terms we may refer to as *relata*. This does not beg the question of the possibility of 'internal' or 'necessary' relations, since it says nothing about the relative ontological statuses of the two *relata*. It is what may be called a 'relation of fact'. And, again, I do not mean by this description to beg the question of logical status, for example, to preempt the title of a natural relation only for contingent, 'matter of fact' relations. I mean, rather, that whatever the logical status of the relation, the claim that it holds is something like an ontological claim.

I want to contrast with this idea of natural relation the idea of a 'relation of meaning'. And in this contrast I am following, to some extent, a distinction made recently by Professor Roy Holland, who writes, 'For the reality of value is not one of fact but of meaning' (see his paper 'Moral Scepticism', *Proc. Arist. Soc. Supp.*, 1967, p. 194). This is not to claim either distinction is yet seen by me at all clearly.

I said earlier that it might make sense to call 'ethical justice' an internal relation—if only we knew clearly what sense *that* made. It may be that the sense of 'internal relation', at least as applied to the concept of ethical justice, goes quite closely with the sense of 'relation of meaning'.

If a natural relation is in some sense an 'objective relation', that is to say, a relation whose holding is independent of its being observed or willed to hold, then we might begin by supposing that at least one feature distinctive of a relation of meaning is that its holding is not independent of its being observed or willed to hold. In this sense, but in this sense only, we might call it a 'subjective relation'.

Another feature, the one hopefully indicated by its name, is that a relation of meaning can be thought of as holding between two things, or states of affairs, etcetera, if and only if it holds between these two elements *for* for some observer or agent, for some human subject. Clearly, the distinction is not yet specific enough. We might try to specify it by saying it applies if and only if for somebody the two elements are significantly (meaningfully) related; that is, if and only if there is some significance (meaning) in the two elements being as they are in respect of one another.

When we speak of a relation of meaning, we are speaking not just of a presumed relation (of whatever sort) between two elements, but of the *sense*, the meaning, or the significance of their having such a relation for him, or what it means for him that he experiences the elements as so related.

The idea of an internal relation does not coincide with this rough explanation. For traditionally an internal relation has been distinguished from a matter-of-fact relation by claiming, for example, that the holding of an internal relation is essential to each of the related objects' being what they are: it is of their essence, an essential attribute of each. However, the holding of an external and matter-of-fact relation is a contingent and accidental matter. By my rough account, an internal relation, as so identified, might well count as a 'relation of fact'. For this identification does not refer at all to what somebody makes of the relation.

Let us turn away from asking why ethical justice should be seen as a good, and ask instead *what*, in the ethical punishment, is good — ethically speaking. Obviously the answer to the latter will illuminate the answer to the former, if it has an answer.

There are a number of suggestions one might make in answer to the question what in the ethical punishment is good. They are all, however, clearly inadequate in terms of my previous analyses. For example, one might say: it is because the ethical punishment occurred, or because it occurred to the wrongdoer. All these are inadequate as answers, since they rely on failing to distinguish the natural occurrence which embodies or expresses an ethical punishment from the ethical punishment. One might, again, say: it is because such-and-such happened to him *as the punishment* for his wrongdoing. This is obviously a better answer, but still unsatisfactory because of the same failure and confusion the other answers revealed.

So let us try including the subject's, or the wrongdoer's, own subjectivity, that is, his apprehension and understanding, into our answer. We might then, for example, claim that what makes the ethical punishment a good is that the wrongdoer recognizes that he did wrong, in ethical terms, and thus that what he did is deserving of punishment. And he recognizes that this punishment is *just* in relation to his wrongdoing.

With this answer we are approaching, I believe, Kierkegaard's own answer, and quite generally beginning to talk sense. But we may feel ourselves facing an antinomy; namely, whether ethical justice is a good in itself, or whether its being a good depends on its being recognized by the 'sufferer' as justice. The antinomy possibly raised by the present answer is not quite this. It is, rather, whether the goodness or ethical justice depends on its being recognized as justice and *ipso facto* as an ethical good, or whether it merely depends on its being recognized as justice, but not received as an ethical good.

Kierkegaard, I believe, tries to build the former point into his answer. A further answer on such Kierkegaardian lines might be that the good of ethical punishment rests in its being recognized and accepted as an ethical good, namely, the ethical good of justice, by the sufferer — that is, in its being accepted by him 'gratefully' as his just punishment.

Both antinomies I cited appear to involve for their solution — if there is one — a careful distinction between *a*, something's being the ethical punishment for someone's wrongdoing, and *b*, something's being accepted by that person as the ethical punishment for wrongdoing. But it is, after all, not clear that we can distinguish *a* from *b*, nor, if so, what the distinction comes to. There seems to be a possible way of connecting them with each other. For it looks as if something's being accepted by me as the ethical punishment for my wrongdoing might be conceived as a sufficient condition for its actually being the punishment, but not as a necessary condition.

Kierkegaard claims that the punishment is a good only when gratefully received (p. 93). This assertion implies, clearly, that when the punishment is not received gratefully — for example, if it is received 'ungratefully' or not received as a punishment at all — it is not a good. Or: when it is not received as a good, it is not a good. This does not mean that when not received as a good it is an evil. For something's not being an ethical good is not sufficient to make it an ethical evil. It may simply not figure on any ethical scale of values. So it is possible that ethical punishment, if not received as a good, might be conceived as simply failing to figure as an ethical value at all, and therefore as failing also to figure as an ethical evil.

What could 'gratefully receiving punishment' mean? First, it must mean acknowledging what one is getting as punishment, that is, as the ethical recompense for one's wrongdoing. And this in turn involves recognizing that one has done wrong, that one's act was an ethical evil. Both these implications involve of necessity an ethical point of view, or an ethical frame of mind. I think there is a third implication too. That is, that one must receive one's acknowledged punishment as the expression of ethical justice. For this is to say no more than that one acknowledges the punishment as rightfully given for one's wrongdoing.

But there is a fourth point too, that is concerned with the gratitude which Kierkegaard claims necessary, if the punishment is to count as a good. To receive something gratefully is to be glad that one is receiving it; that is, the receiving of it means the satisfaction of one's desire or will. So to receive punishment gratefully means that the punishment is the satisfaction of one's desire or will. And that means the punishment is what one desires or wills. It may well be, for all I can see, that one is supposed to desire or will the punishment in its aspect as the expression of justice, since from the ethical point of view justice is certainly a desirable thing, or something to be willed.

One might wonder, now, what distinguishes receiving punishment with gratitude from receiving the ethical reward, for both appear to be taken as ethical goods.

It cannot be that the ethical punishment is some kind of natural harm, while the ethical reward is some kind of natural good, like wealth or fame. For there is no such correlation of necessity. It may even be the case, for example, that a man does wrong and as a consequence gets rich. Now he may not think in the ethical mode at all. But he may, and if he does, he may conceivably see his wealth not as the ethical reward, but as the ethical punishment for his wrongdoing. Vice versa, the saint may conceivably receive his earthly martyrdom not as the ethical punishment, but as the ethical reward for his virtue.

So presumably the idea of ethical punishment must be the idea of some kind of 'ethical harm', and the idea of ethical reward the idea of some kind of 'ethical welfare' — however these ideas are to be understood. But then we need to ask what kind of ethical harm such a punishment could be.

There seems only one possible answer. For there seems only one possible interpretation of the idea of an *ethical* harm. And that is the idea of the ethical harm that comes to a man in and from his wrongdoing; for example, that condition of the soul or ethical self which gives rise to wrongdoing, is expressed in wrongdoing, and which wrongdoing fortifies and strengthens. Plausibly, such conditions are seen when, for example, a man becomes (is) evil or morally weak, or when, perhaps, he loses his ethical selfhood, for example, in madness or bestiality.

Certainly this answer would also yield an easy and plausible explanation of the internality of the relation between wrongdoing and its ethical punishment. For the connections envisaged here are not merely causal ones.

And it might explain my idea that this relation is a 'relation of meaning', itself identified by ethical criteria. And, more important, it is only for someone whose perception of events falls within the ethical mode that any relation between wrongdoing and punishment could even make sense. And, finally, for such a person this relationship, being, as I argued, the relationship of ethical justice, can be called 'meaningful' — a relation of meaning — in a preeminent sense. For the idea of ethical justice, as I have tried to explain, is certainly one of those ideas that are cardinal in constituting and patterning his whole vision of life by giving its peculiarly ethical 'shape' or meaning to life as he experiences it.

But, if this is the correct solution, it appears to leave us with a hard paradox. For we are already committed to claiming that the ethical individual will be capable of receiving his punishment with gratitude, that is, as a good. Now it is plain that it might be received as the manifestation of justice. One may recognize one's own moral degeneration, for example, as the 'just' consequence of one's own wrongdoing. But it is not so plain how the ethical individual could recognize his own moral degeneration as an ethical *good*. How could he *desire* ethical harm for himself? How could he possibly desire to become worse, even if he became so as a result of his own wrongdoing?

CHAPTER 5

The unity of the good

f it is to be possible, that a man can will only one thing, then he must will the Good' (*Purity of Heart*, p. 53).

Kierkegaard later repeats and emphasizes his point: 'FOR IN TRUTH TO WILL ONE THING, A MAN MUST WILL THE GOOD'. This was the first point, *the possibility of being able to will one thing*. But in order 'GENUINELY TO WILL ONE THING, A MAN MUST IN TRUTH WILL THE GOOD' (pp. 121–22). And in the earlier section he comments, 'For the Good without condition and without qualification, without preface and without compromise is, absolutely the only thing that a man may and should will, and is only one thing' (p. 54).

This is one of the many aspects of Kierkegaard's moral philosophy which suggests a subjectivist interpretation. But it is plain to anyone who reads him sympathetically that 'subjectivism' is too simple a concept to fit his philosophy accurately. This does not imply that we may in reaction simply call him an 'objectivist'. His ideas are too complex and subtle for these contemporary labels.

I want to consider some aspects (not all) of Kierkegaard's concept of 'purity of heart', and to bring out how a proper use of this concept enables him to successfully avoid the charge of subjectivism, or at least subjectivism at the points indicated by my citations.

Since Kant we have grown used to distinguishing moralities of autonomy from moralities of heteronomy. The distinction is not clear or distinct, but will serve for the purpose I want to put it to.

Roughly, we can say a heteronomy-morality is one in which the idea of the Good is the idea of an independent object, that is, one which subsists and is definable independently of the idea of the 'good will'. So the 'good will' may be defined, formally, as 'the will whose true object is the Good'. Similarly, an autonomy-morality is one in which, conversely, the idea of an ethical good (if not necessarily any idea of some good) is defined partly in terms of the idea of the good will. So, for example, 'the Good' may be defined as 'the true object of the good will'.

It is here that subjectivism offers itself as a plausible interpretation, perhaps a pressing one. For how, one wants to ask, can it make sense to speak of an 'objective' Good, if that good is definable simply in terms of a particular mode of the human will? Nor can we appeal to the prior notion of the particular goodness of the good will. For there does not seem to be any external standard, so to speak, against which the human will may be measured to determine its goodness or badness. So one may even, at this point, wonder what sense it makes to speak of a 'good' will.

It is necessary to remember throughout this discussion that I am talking only about autonomy-moralities. For, of course, it is very easy for a heteronomist to give an account of the goodness of the good will. There are many external standards he can use for this purpose.

Kierkegaard is, on the surface I think, so plainly an autonomist that just these difficulties I have been describing are characteristic of his work too. They may be summed up by observing that he appears to want to assert the theses both of the morality of autonomy and of objectivism. He wants, it seems, both to claim that the idea of the Good is definable only in terms of the idea of the human will in some particular mode and to claim that it is the idea of something independent of any mode or condition of the human will. And these two claims appear to be contradictory.

I can now reformulate my aim in these kinds of terms. I want to show that these two claims are not necessarily contradictory, and that Kierkegaard provides us with a way of reconciling them. And that is by the concept of 'purity of heart'. For this is the concept of a particular mode of the will in which alone the Good is the will's true object, and by reference to which alone the idea of the Good can be defined. But it is also a concept which allows that idea to retain the kind of independence necessary for its 'objectivity'.

We might also say that in the concept of 'purity of heart'

there is implicitly contained that reference to an 'external standard' which allows sense to the idea of the good will, that is, to the idea of the goodness of the good will, while retaining the framework of autonomism.

Before discussing Kierkegaard's views, I want briefly to introduce a conceptual distinction which I shall later use in explaining these views.

Philosophers have sometimes distinguished the categories of 'mental act', 'object of a mental act', and 'content of a mental act'. For example, they have distinguished the ideas of the act of will (the willing), the object of that act (the object of one's willing), and the content of that act. It must be admitted that the latter idea, the content of the act, is hard to understand.

To understand Kierkegaard's views on the will we must certainly make use of the traditional distinction between the act of willing and its object. But we must, I believe, also introduce a further distinction. (Perhaps this can be interpreted as a way of making the distinction between the act of willing and its content. Perhaps not.) This is the distinction between the act of willing and its *mode* or *manner*. (I am not even sure that we should not further distinguish between the mode of willing and its manner.)

Two possible examples of the idea of the will's mode or manner are the strength or weakness of one's will, for example, the degree of one's determination or the strength of one's commitment, and the unity, or internal consistency, as opposed to the multiplicity, or internal conflict, of one's will.

The correct conceptual place of these examples is not clear to me, and I do not claim that I have certainly found it. But it does seem quite clear that the strength or weakness of one's will may be distinguished from the mere act of willing itself and also from the object of will. And it does not seem easy to subsume such characteristics under the idea of the 'content' of the will, whatever this is.

The importance of a distinction such as the one I have introduced is, briefly, this. Traditionally, the ideas of the act of will and of its object (or content) have been taken as logically independent. Now if they are logically independent, there can be no possible way of inferring from the mere occurrence of an act of will what its object is in itself, nor under what intentional descriptions it falls—with the trivial exception of the description 'thing willed'. It follows at once that there can be no possibility of inferring the moral character of that object. In other words, the moral character of the object of will is independent of the occurrence of the act.

But it is not possible to argue in the same way that the ideas of the object of will and the manner of the willing (the mode of the act) are logically independent, although I think what amounts to this conclusion has sometimes been erroneously drawn from the quite different premisses described just above. For we cannot hold that the manner of willing is independent of the object of the will. 'Object of the will' is an ambiguous phrase, however, and this last claim cannot be made clear and plausible until the ambiguity is exposed. It is a familiar enough ambiguity, however. For it is simply the distinction between the idea of the object of will as it is in itself, and the idea of the object of will as it is for the will; for example, as it occurs in the 'intentional description' under which it is presented to the willing subject.

The manner of willing, then, is clearly, we may suppose, independent of the actual nature or character of the object of will in itself. But it does not follow that it is independent of the nature and character of the 'intentional object'. Indeed, and this is my claim repeated, it is not independent of it.

And I further claim that it is upon this logical interdependence of the object of will and the manner of the willing that Kierkegaard partly builds his bridge between subjectivity and objectivity. These last pages have been admittedly schematic. So I shall now turn to the actual concepts used by Kierkegaard.

'Only the Good is one thing *in its essence* and the same in each of its expressions' (p. 60: my italics). This is the claim on which he rests virtually the whole of the ethical-religious doctrine of *Purity of Heart*. Other quotations show us in somewhat different terms the same claim. 'Shall a man in truth will one thing, then this one thing that he wills must be such that that *it remains unaltered in all changes*, so that by willing it he can win immutability' (p. 60: my italics). He adds, 'If . . . a man should in truth will only one thing, then this thing must, *in the truth of its innermost being*, be one thing' (p. 66: my italics).

Let us express these claims in the following words. The Good is an 'essential unity'. The idea of 'the Good', that is, the absolute Good, is the idea, at least, of an essential unity. 'Essential unity', whatever it means, may be contrasted with 'accidental unity', whatever this means. So Kierkegaard may be construed as claiming, at least, that the idea of the absolute Good is the idea of something which is a 'unity' not accidentally but essentially.

These are dark claims, although illuminated (I believe) by passages from Plato and Saint Augustine. And this is not the place to make a deep or exhaustive analysis of their precise sense. I am afraid that for my present purpose I shall just have to take it that those meanings, which I have described above, and which are not clear, but yet not intolerably vague, can be assigned to Kierkegaard's words. And those meanings are to be attributed to these claims whenever they occur below.

If the Good is defined as at least an essential unity, it follows that the idea of 'willing the Good' must be at least the idea of 'willing an essential unity'. Now this is a definition which does not commit its author to autonomy-morality or subjectivism. For it can be given a perfectly good sense within heteronomism. For example, we might define the idea of the good will as the idea of a will whose object is an essential unity (perhaps the one essential unity). It still rests upon us, in this case, to give a clear indication of what is meant by an 'essential unity'. But nothing prevents that indication in principle.

Unity is a concept, however, which Kierkegaard applies not only to the idea of the Good, that is, to something which is a possible object of the will. It is a concept which he applies also to the will itself.

We speak of 'single-mindedness'. Kierkegaard prefers to speak of its opposite, 'double-mindedness'. Both ideas involve application of the formal concept of unity to the will. We might also speak of a 'single will' or a 'double will'. I think that sometimes Kierkegaard uses the expression 'willing one thing in truth' to refer to single-mindedness, or singleness of the will. This is confusing, if I am right, since it is an expression which could also be quite naturally used to refer to the formal character of the will's object, just as 'willing one thing' is used. Nevertheless, I think that the addition of those crucially Kierkegaardian words 'in truth' signifies that we are now considering not the object of the will but, so to speak, the subject.

Now there is no autonomist definition of 'the Good' that exactly parallels the heteronomist definition of the good will I gave. But we can provide one which uses, instead, the concept of the unity of the will. For we can simply define the Good as 'the object of the unified will', that is, as the object of a single will. If I am right in my guess about Kierkegaard's terminology, then we may also define the Good as 'the object of that will which wills one thing in truth'. (And this will not now be a tautology.)

However, it is just at this point that subjectivism enters the garden. For it does not seem absurd to suppose that a man might possess a will that was directed single-mindedly upon some one object, while that object was still of a kind we should want to call evil. Putting the objection in the more familiar idiom of 'sincerity', we may, it appears, easily suppose that someone sincerely wills an evil end. And the difficulty appears now to be that the autonomist is unable, using language in its normal sense, to say anything like this. The statement must represent a self-contradiction for him. So, faced by a situation or image of this kind, he must either contradict himself (or perhaps even withdraw his definition of the Good), or claim, contrary to normal understanding, that the man's sincerity does after all suffice to show that the object of his will is 'good'. (Compare, for example, the concept of 'the sincere Nazi'.)

If one thing is clear about Kierkegaard's ethical views, it is that he was not an autonomist, if by being an autonomist we mean someone whose conception of the Good and the good will, and their relations, commits him to these conclusions. But it is precisely where he diverges from simple autonomism that we have to discover. And this is not easy.

We are inclined to say that whether or not the will is itself unified is irrelevant to the nature or character of its object. To be unified is merely a mode of the act of willing (although a peculiar one). It is not a mode of the object of the will.

Now I suggested earlier that the opinion that the mode of the willing and the character of the object of will are logically independent of each other is not correct. I do not mean to demonstrate this in general. But I want here to suggest that it is false at any rate with respect to that peculiar mode I have called unity.

What the subjectivist wishes to claim is that there is nothing in the concept of the unity of the act of willing, that is, in the concept of single-mindedness or sincerity, which has any consequences for or restrictions on possible objects of the will. So a man can, so to speak, sincerely and single-mindedly pursue many quite different sorts of object. Then, we might reasonably object, are these all to be identified as the Good? Indeed, since sincerity is not apparently itself a sufficient criterion for the moral goodness of the object sincerely pursued, where has the idea of 'morality' gone?

Kierkegaard claims, and I believe rightly so, that there is a necessary connection between the ideas of the unity of the act of willing and the unity of the object of will. And this claim involves use of the concept of 'essential' unity once more.

'If . . . a man should in truth will only one thing, then this thing must, in the truth of its innermost being, be one thing' (p. 66). Conversely, *'In truth to will one thing, then, can only mean to will the Good*, because every other object is not a unity; and the will that only wills that object, therefore, must become double-minded. For as the coveted object is, so becomes the coveter' (p. 66: my italics). Here Kierkegaard clearly has to be understood as claiming that if the object of the will is not an essential unity, the act of will itself cannot be a unity either. It is not enough that the object be an accidental unity. This, I believe, is shown in the remark: 'Shall a man in truth will one thing, then this one thing that he wills must be such that it remains unaltered in all changes, so that by willing it he can win immutability. If it changes continually, then he himself becomes changeable, double-minded, and unstable' (p. 60). And similarly, 'The person who wills one thing that is not the Good, he does not truly will one thing. . . . For in his innermost being he is, he is bound to be, double-minded' (p. 55).

In my terms, Kierkegaard is claiming that essential unity of the act of willing is impossible without an essential unity of the object of the will. Or: single-mindedness, sincerity, is impossible unless directed upon an essential unity. That is also to say, that if the object of the will is merely accidentally a unity, it cannot be willed single-mindedly. The act of willing whose object it is cannot be itself a unity, but must be multiple.

Thus, we might say, for Kierkegaard the question of the sense and application of the concept 'the absolute Good' involves, if it is not equivalent to, the question of the sense and application of the concept 'an essential unity'. And to justify the implicit claim that the Good is unique, he must also show that the concept of 'essential unity' can apply only to one entity, and that it does apply to the concept of the Good.

Now in the passage I quoted just above, Kierkegaard illustrates the concept of 'essential unity' by the notions of change, alteration, mutability, and instability. These, as ordinarily understood, are notions involving the ordinary notion of time. Contrasted with them are such 'nontemporal' notions as rest, permanence, immutability, and stability. And it is through these notions that

Kierkegaard illustrates and explains his concept of 'essential unity'. In a word, through his notion of 'eternity'.

So his arguments for the uniqueness of the essential unity of the Good revolve around the contrast, or the dichotomy, between the orders of time and eternity: the temporal and the eternal. This is not to say that he explains the notion of the eternal, and then uses that notion to explain the concept of essential unity. He does not. The notion of the eternal remains mysterious, for it is a 'transcendental' notion. Rather, he considers the notions of time and temporal existence, and certain of their most central characteristics. And this consideration illustrates the concept of a merely 'accidental' unity by giving some content to the concept of 'accidentality'.

For Kierkegaard, the notions of time or the temporal and 'the world' are intimately connected. And by 'the world' he simply means the actual world of facts and (maybe) natural necessities in which we live: everything that is an actual or possible object of ordinary sense-perception and scientific theorizing. If we use the concept of actuality for this world, we can put his theses in this way: everything actual is temporal, and has the necessary attributes of whatever exists in time, whatever these may be.

I do not want to go deeply into his arguments here. But it is necessary, all the same, to sketch their main outlines, their gist, their drive.

Kierkegaard names several 'worldly' ends. And by 'ends' I do not mean particular objects of the will as they are in themselves. I mean, rather, types of intentional object. For example, he names pleasure, honour, the great and 'great moments', strength of will, the evil, and the impressive. (Later, I shall bring out the special importance of the two notions of greatness and strength.)

There are three kinds of argument which he uses to show that none of these worldly goals, nor more generally any worldly goal, can be a unity in its essence.

First, he argues that all such goals are essentially changeable. 'It is not, nor does it remain one thing, while everything else is in change or while he himself is in change. It is not in all circumstances the same. On the contrary, it is subject to continual alteration' (p. 56).

He argues, too, that all such goals are essentially not ones but manifolds: such a thing as, say, pleasure, 'is in itself a multitude of things, a dispersion, the toy of changeableness, and the prey of corruption' (p. 56). A man for whom the object of his will is pleasure has a will which is thereby set on a form of variety and diversity.

These arguments are both familiar and antique. They go back at least to Plato. So, I think, does the next.

Kierkegaard claims, more radically, that no 'worldly' goal can be *real*. 'The fact is that the worldly goal is not one thing in its essence because it is unreal. Its so-called unity is actually nothing but emptiness which is hidden beneath the manyness' (pp. 59–60).

This is clearly a general claim about the 'ontological status' of things like pleasure, worldly honour, and greatness. It is, apparently, the claim that suchlike things *have no essence* at all. So what their names name are merely appearances. So, for example, the name 'pleasure' names nothing but a number of contingently grouped phenomena. And the unity of this grouping must be not only contingent but subjective. For since there is nothing, so to speak, behind and within the manifold phenomena in virtue of which each phenomenon of this group is properly to be called 'pleasure', the only principle of grouping that we can be using is a purely subjective one—if it can be called a principle at all.

I would not say that Kierkegaard argues from the claim that, say, pleasure has no essence to the claim that it must be a subjective phenomenon. Probably he argues the other way around. And this too would be a respectable and traditional form of argument, again going back to Plato if not beyond. Moreover, from the premiss that pleasure names a subjective phenomenon also follow the two earlier claims: that it is essentially changeable and essentially a manifold.

There are two other kinds of argument which he uses to show that no worldly goal can be a unity in its essence. One is presented in these words. 'Carried to its extreme limit, what is pleasure other than disgust? What is earthly honour at its dizzy pinnacle other than contempt for existence? What are riches, the highest superabundance of riches, other than poverty? ... What is worldly omnipotence other than dependence? What slave in chains is as unfree as a tyrant!' (p. 60). Part of the idea is obviously that worldly states are all too apt not to last. Pleasure becomes disgust; fame breeds ennui; wealth vanishes and leaves poverty. These are commonplaces of stoical philosophizing. But Kierkegaard is, I believe, saying more than just this. His words seem to imply that this sort of change is somehow necessary. That is, that there is what might be called a 'dialectic' of pleasure, or honour, or power. This is not a merely silly claim.

The most familiar example of this 'dialectic' of concepts concerns the concepts of freedom and power. Thinking about these things in the ordinary way, we might say: the more power (worldly power), the more freedom. But a philosophically familiar line of thought now counters: the more worldly power, the less *true* freedom. And this answer rests upon the use of a quite different, and partly opposed, concept of 'freedom'. Generally, it might be answered: the more freedom in the world's sense of freedom, the less true freedom. A similar example can easily be constructed for the concept of pleasure: this too is traditional and Platonising. The more worldly pleasure, the less 'true pleasure'. And again, the more worldly honour, the less 'true honour'. The more worldly riches, the less 'true riches'. And so on.

If I am right, this argument is closely connected with Kierkegaard's third argument that nothing worldly can be an essential unity. And both these arguments are associated with the idea that nothing worldly is 'real'. 'Diverse as it is, in life it is changed into its opposite, in death into nothing, in eternity into damnation: for the one who has willed this goal' (p. 60). An essential unity would not be capable in life of being changed into its opposite, and it would not be capable of simply vanishing at death into nothing.

It seems that here we can find an answer. For surely death represents the end of all human experience, or human life; and, if this is so, then the fact that something 'vanishes' does not in the least prove that it vanishes into nothing. It proves only what has been admitted, that we are no longer capable of any kind of experience or conscious relation to it.

However, I think Kierkegaard is here relying implicitly on his principle of homogeneity or 'harmony': 'as the coveted object is, so becomes the coveter' (p. 66). For this principle immediately implies that to be capable of truly willing some goal, a man must himself be sufficiently like that goal; that is, his will must share some important feature of that goal. Ontologically speaking, it implies that a man's will must be or become like its object. So to be able to will worldly and temporal objects, a man must have a worldly and temporal will, or nature: to be able to will nontemporal and eternal objects, for example, the Good, a man's will must be in part nontemporal and eternal. 'Shall a man in truth will one thing, then this one thing that he wills must be such that it remains unaltered in all changes, *so that by willing it he can win immutability*. If it changes continually, *then he himself becomes changeable, doubleminded, and unstable*' (p. 60: my italics). And he later adds that the 'one thing' will 'fashion that man who only wills one thing into conformity with itself' (p. 66).

Now the ideas of 'essential unity' and 'eternity' are explicitly connected in one passage. Kierkegaard says, of the essential unity, that 'It must, by *an eternal separation*, cut off the heterogeneous from itself in order that *it may in truth continue to be one and the same thing*' (p. 66: my italics).

'Eternity' here, as always in Kierkegaard, signifies at least a distinction of *category*. So, for example, it signifies that it is not merely wrong, but nonsensical, to speak of, say, 'eternal' happiness in terms appropriate to ordinary happiness. The most familiar category-distinction of the kind which Kierkegaard is using is,

perhaps, the Kantian distinction between 'natural goods' and 'moral goods', or the realms of necessity and freedom.

Kierkegaard's arguments, if they are valid, go to prove that no worldly, that is, temporal, entity can possibly be an essential unity. And so, if we accept the principle of homogeneity of the will and its object, they go to suggest that no act of will which is set upon a temporal entity can be itself 'essentially' unified. Now this is not to say that such a will might not be unified. For it might be, so to speak, accidentally, or contingently, unified. But what 'unifies' it is now the merely contingent unity of its object; that is, a unity which is merely phenomenal, which is essentially liable to change, which lacks an essential basis, and which cannot significantly be said to survive death.

The possessor of a will which is contingently unified, or, more precisely, the subject of such a will, must therefore himself be liable to the same kinds of change as his will. That is to say, he cannot be himself any more than a merely temporal existent. He is, indeed, what we ordinarily conceive human beings to be: a certain kind of temporal entity, appearing at one time, disappearing at another period, between these two times of 'birth' and 'death', and enjoying a mode of activity and consciousness that is called 'life', including the appreciation and pursuit of various objects or goals.

Kierkegaard, of course, thinks of man as not simply a denizen of this world, but also a denizen of 'eternity'. In traditional theological terms, he thinks man possesses, or possesses the potentiality of gaining, immortality, or 'eternal life'. We do not have to think of his point in theological terms, however. I think we can construe it, rather, in terms of the Kantian ethics. (I do not claim that this interpretation gives Kierkegaard's thoughts their full value. Of course it cannot, since his philosophy differs from Kant's in respect of the relations between ethics and theology. But I think this interpretation may serve as a guide to the proper understanding of Kierkegaard.)

To be a merely natural subject, in terms such as those I used just above to describe the ordinary conception of human being, is not yet to be an *ethical subject*. It is this concept that Kierkegaard is using. Man is, for him, not merely a natural subject, but an ethical subject, a being subject to ethical claims and ethical ideals. (He is also a 'religious subject', but that is a matter I am not here explicitly discussing.) And the sense in which he is an ethical subject is very like the sense in which for Kant man is an ethical subject, besides being a natural subject.

If a man lives a merely natural life, that is, exists as a natural subject and no more, then his will can be directed only upon 'natural objects', and can have only the unity appropriate to and possible for natural objects. And that is contingent and temporary unity. Then the same will hold for the man, the subject, himself.

If there is to be any essential unity, it must be something belonging to the ethical (or religious) realm. And if a man's will is to acquire essential unity, it must be directed onto such an ethical (or religious) object.

So far I have not shown that there can be only one ethical object and thus that there cannot be more than one essential unity.

Now one might try to take the short way, and simply say that the idea of the (ethical) good is such a unique ethical object. And there is a sense in this claim. For certainly it can be claimed that 'the good' is the name of that 'intentional object' of the will, that is, that description under which all particular objects of the will must fall. Perhaps 'good' is too wide a concept to define the ethical. Rather, we should think of the idea of the 'absolute' or 'unconditional' good, as Kierkegaard himself does. Still, if 'unconditional' good names the intentional object of the distinctively ethical will, it remains true that the particular objects of the will are many and various. And this is what gives force to subjectivism. The short-cut answer will not distinguish Kierkegaard's position from subjectivism.

I think at this point we probably have to return to the idea of the 'essentially unified' will, and consider what its object (or objects) could possibly be. It is clear, right off, that it must be a species of the ethical will. Now to claim that there can be only one species of the ethical will looks like begging the very question at issue, or rather making the same mistake as was made just above. For this explanation helps no more than, say, the concept of sincerity helps towards generating or safeguarding anything recognizable as an ethical 'objectivity'. As far as that goes, indeed, we might simply claim that sincerity is a mark of, or a criterion for, the ethical will. What is needed to substantiate the claim that there is an ethical objectivity is the claim that there is *an ethical object*. (Remember that we are considering only autonomy-ethics.)

At this point let me recapitulate my exposition of Kierkegaard's argument, as I have reconstructed it. The problem is set by Kierkegaard's desire to construct an ethics that is autonomous but objective. This looks like an impossible task, since it demands that the Good should be defined by reference to the concept of the good will but at the same time remain an objective concept. In this aim the formal concept of unity plays a central part. 'The Good' is to be an essential unity, and the good will an essentially unified or single will. Now, introducing the traditional idea of the act of will and its object, and the untraditional idea of the manner or mode of willing, Kierkegaard claims a necessary relation between the unity of the object of will and the unifiedness of the act of will, that is, its mode as unitary. This does not yet get him out of the dark forest of subjectivism, obviously, since it may be admitted that a unified will is a necessary and sufficient condition of the moral will, while claiming that such a will can have many, perhaps indefinitely many, possible objects. At this point, then, the distinction between the ideas of 'essential unity' and 'accidental unity' becomes crucial. Kierkegaard illustrates the idea of an accidental unity by referring to some necessary features of temporal (actual) existence, for example, change, or, more precisely, changeability. All temporal existence, and therefore all actual objects of the will, must be mere contingent unities — if they are unities at all. And the subject whose will is directed upon such objects can be itself no more than a contingently unified subject; he can be no more than contingently single-minded. So, if there can be any essential unity or any essentially single will ('willing one thing in truth'), it must be a nontemporal, that is, 'eternal', object, and its subject must be in some sense 'eternal' too. The distinction between the realms of time and eternity can be indicated, though not fully exemplified, in the Kantian distinction between the realms of nature and morality (freedom), and between man considered as a natural (phenomenal) subject and man considered as an ethical subject (intelligible, transcendental). So the essentially single will must be, at least, something like a Kantian ethical will. (I am not here arguing for what I should elsewhere claim to be able to show; namely, that Kierkegaard's own Christian ethics is in fact built on Kantian foundations.) Obviously this has not solved the original problem, since precisely one of the distinctive features of Kantian ethics is its abjuration of the idea of there being any *object*, such as the Good might be. (We should however remember that reason provides us with and practically justifies the *ideas* of God and immortality, etcetera.)

It may look as if the argument has merely brought us round in a great circle to our starting point. But I do not think this is so. For it has introduced into our minds a number of concepts which, I believe, will help to offer a genuine solution. That is, help to justify a genuinely objectivist autonomy-ethics. But the cardinal concept has not yet been put to use. It is the concept of 'purity of heart'.

To think that Kierkegaard's doctrine is 'autonomous' in the sense that his concept of the good must be empty or purely formal, as is Kant's, is to suppose that Kierkegaard's ethics gives the same ethical grounds to *fanaticism* as it does to the concept of the good will. It is to suppose that Kierkegaard's explanation of the concept of the good will, arguably like Kant's (and certainly like

Sartre's), is such that it cannot possibly accommodate a distinction between the concepts of 'good will' and 'fanatical will'.

This roughly sums up the standard objection that no autonomy-ethics can accommodate an ethical objectivity. And I shall now try to show that, contrary to appearances, the distinction between the concepts of good will and fanatical will can in fact be made very clearly within Kierkegaard's ethics, and how the possibility of making this distinction amounts to successfully making room for ethical objectivity within that ethics.

CHAPTER 6

The concept 'purity of heart'

There are several related distinctions Kierkegaard uses in order to distinguish his 'objectivist' autonomy-ethics from subjectivism. They are: (1) the distinction between the idea of single-mindedness in the sense of exclusiveness, hardness, and insensitivity, and the idea of the 'loving will'; (2) the distinction between the ideas of willing what is great, that is, 'enthusiasm', and willing what is good; and (3) the distinction between nonethical concepts of human weakness and strength and the ethicoreligious concepts of sin (evil) and purity (goodness), implying a distinction between the idea that weakness is a misfortune but strength a good, and the idea that sin is 'corruption', and purity 'salvation'. I want to go through these distinctions and try to bring out some of the points I conceive Kierkegaard to be making, and some of the connections between these points.

1 / 'For in truth there was a man on earth who seemed to will only one thing. It was unnecessary for him to insist upon it. Even if he had been silent about it, there were witnesses enough against him who testified how inhumanly he steeled his mind, how nothing touched him, neither tenderness, nor innocence, nor misery; how his blinded soul had eyes for nothing, and how the senses in him had only eyes for the one thing that he willed' (p. 56). And yet, Kierkegaard goes on, it was a terrible delusion that he willed one thing.

His actual argument appears to be that this kind of single-mindedness is directed upon worldly objects, and is thus subject to the changeability and lack of essential unity of the worldly in general.

But there is obviously an implicit distinction at work within the very terms of his description: 'how inhumanly he steeled his mind', 'how nothing touched him', 'tenderness', 'misery', and so forth. The picture is not simply the picture of single-minded willing. It is a picture of a will that is inhuman, fanatical. Its inhumanity is expressed in the will's emotional and moral insensitivity, or rather willed suspension of sensitivity, and in its intellectual blindness. I do not claim these are distinct or independent.

One might also describe this will as hardhearted. The main point is that the single-mindedness of such a man's willing is expressed in his *exclusively* willing just that one object, whatever it is. And thus his will is more or less deliberately turned away from, and excludes any other object, such as human misery or innocence. Generally, it is turned away from other human beings.

Thus Kierkegaard is implying that single-mindedness need not necessarily be taken to involve this sort of exclusiveness, that is, to exclude consideration of other people. How is this possible? It is possible, clearly, only on condition that the 'formal' object of such a single-minded will is such as to include other people and their 'innocence' and 'misery'; that is, such as to necessarily involve the possibility of humanity, compassion, and tenderness. That is to say, the single-minded will is also what might be called a *loving* will, where the lovingness is not accidental to the will but essential to it.

Now I think Kierkegaard is not arguing merely that the idea of single-mindedness does not necessarily entail the qualities of inhumanity, blindness, etcetera. I think he wants also to argue that, properly understood, it rules them out. 'Willing one thing *in truth*' (my italics), as he would say, if properly understood can be seen to entail the qualities of humanity and love.

And he seems also to be arguing that the unloving will is only apparently willing one thing: that the single-mindedness of fanaticism, let us call it, is only an apparent singleness. Perhaps we should say rather that the singlemindedness of fanaticism can be no more than accidental singleness. So only the single-mindedness of the loving will can be an essential singleness, or unity.

The fanatical will must be exclusive. The fanatic's actions must be directed to only this one object, and all other aims and values must be neglected. Everything other than the one object of his will must be sacrificed for the achievement of this object.

If there is to be a condition of the will in which single-mindedness does not necessarily involve the possibility of 'sacrificing' the good and happiness of other human beings for the achievement of the will's object, it can clearly only be one in which the will's object is, or includes, the good and happiness of other human beings. Only on this condition can the good and happiness of others be relevant to the will. But, of course, in such a condition the will's single-mindedness *must* involve pursuit of the good and happiness of others.

Now 'the good and happiness of others' must be understood as the good and happiness of all others, of all human beings. But it is not clear what this good and happiness amounts to, nor what I meant by calling such a will a 'loving' will.

We may all agree that generally speaking the ideas of 'love' and 'desire for the good and happiness of' may be identified. (Incidentally, this at once makes it plain that I am not here speaking of anything like the emotional condition characteristic of being in love or falling in love. Rather, what is in question is the ethicoreligious concept of love: *agape*.)

'Good and happiness' cannot be taken in any 'worldly' sense, for example, in any merely empirical or naturalistic sense. For then the question what each person's good and happiness was might admit of different answers at different times, while certainly there would be a vast number of different objects in which such values would reside. So the will directed merely upon these goods and happinesses would be enormously split.

Thus, if there is to be the possibility of a will directed upon the good and happiness of all human beings (or something including this) which is, at the same time, an essential unity, the idea of 'the good and happiness of all human beings' must be understood in a quite different way. It must, for one thing, itself be understood as an essentially single thing—an essential unity. (By 'thing' I do not of course necessarily mean object, that is, piece of matter or condition of the mind or the body.)

As the idea of love involved is an ethical or religious idea, so the ideas of the good and happiness of human beings must also be understood in an ethical or religious (ethicoreligious) sense.

2 / 'Now, willing one thing does not mean to commit the grave

mistake of a brazen, unholy enthusiasm, namely, to will the big, no matter whether it be good or bad' (p. 61).

Much of Kierkegaard's argument rests, I have indicated, on a fundamental distinction between the realms of the ethical and the nonethical. An instance of this is the distinction between the concepts 'great' and 'good'. We are to consider the import of a distinction between the ethical idea of willing the good and the nonethical ('aesthetic'?) idea of 'willing the great'. (Considering the latter idea distinctly from the former idea of hardheartedness does not imply that the two are necessarily distinct or unrelated.)

Now greatness is an idea with at least two different applications. For it can apply, as above, to the object of the will. But it can also be applied to the subject of the willing, when understood as the name of a personal quality, or mark of the personality: compare the concept of 'genius'. It will be in order, then, to consider at once the third notion introduced by Kierkegaard.

3 / This is a distinction between (i) the ideas of human weakness and human strength, and (ii) the ethical ideas of sin and purity of heart, together with the claims (a) that weakness is a human misfortune, an evil for a man, while strength is a man's human salvation, that is, his greatness, and (b) that sin is corruption, while purity of heart is salvation.

It is obvious enough that the distinction is marked quite generally if we say that the ideas (i) and claims (a) are nonethical, while the ideas (ii) and claims (b) are ethical.

Kierkegaard, very roughly, is claiming that it is an error to confuse ideas (i) and (ii), and to confuse claims (a) and (b). They are distinct and, in particular, there is a sense and application to the ethical ones which means that anyone who believes there is sense only to the nonethical ones is mistaken. And this is not just a mistake of fact or logic. It is a 'misperception' of ethics. In fact, from a certain point of view, it is the signal of a total failure to perceive the ethical (a certain region of the ethical) for what it is.

We should distinguish the claim that weakness is a human evil from the claim that sin is corruption, that is, an ethical (ethicoreligious) evil. For only in the latter does 'evil' have an ethical sense. Similarly, we should distinguish the claim that strength is a human good from the claim that purity is a man's salvation, that is, his ethicoreligious good. For only in the latter does 'good' have an ethicoreligious sense.

It can indeed be said that, humanly speaking, strength of will is a good and weakness of will an evil. But to say this is not to say that strength of will is an ethically desirable quality, or that weakness of will is an ethically undesirable quality. (Still less, should we distinguish between them, that either is a religious value.)

Similarly, the idea that 'the Good' names the true object of the truly single-minded will can be interpreted in two ways, according to our understanding of the Good in an ethicoreligious sense or in a nonethical sense. And I have, in effect, argued that there is reason to confuse the ideas of greatness and goodness, 'the great' and 'the good'. For the great might very well be identified with the good, where this is taken in the nonethical sense. That is, the nonethical good might very well be identified with the idea of the great.

So the opinion that Kierkegaard's doctrine of the single-minded will (like Kant's, perhaps) supports fanaticism or enthusiasm, that is, an ethics of the fanatic or the enthusiast, relies on a failure to see that Kierkegaard draws a rigid and uncrossable barrier between the realms of the ethical and the nonethical, and that his claim is made in, and concerning, the language and concepts of the ethical, and explicitly in contrast with the language and concepts of the nonethical. (All this presupposes the possibility of both making such a category-distinction, and showing that the concepts falling within the ethical category, particularly those used by Kierkegaard [and Kant], have a sense and application. And this may be denied.)

Let me repeat the point. Kierkegaard is claiming that the good will is the pure will: the idea of the good will is the idea of the pure will, the idea of 'purity of heart'. He is explicitly not claiming that the good will (the ethically good will) is the strong will. Now someone who fails to see, or make, this sort of distinction cannot make sense of the point I have been emphasizing. For him, perhaps, the idea of the will's 'purity' can mean nothing, unless it means its pure single-mindedness, that is, its fanatical exclusiveness, or its pure enthusiasm, that is, its self-denial before the idea of greatness.

On the other hand, if we allow the concept of purity an independent (and ethical) reality, we can distinguish *two* dimensions of difference to which the human will may be subject. One is an ethical dimension, one is not. (And here we are considering what, in chapter five, I called the manner or mode of the will.) The two dimensions will be the dimension of purity and 'impurity' (sin), and the dimension of strength and weakness.

We shall then be able to distinguish *four* conceptual types: the pure and strong will (corresponding, perhaps, to Kant's concept of the holy, or angelic, will); the pure weak will, that is, the Kierkegaardian concept of the good human being — the saint, maybe; the impure but strong will, which Kierkegaard seems to call the fanatical will; and the impure and weak will, which is, I suppose, characteristic of the normal, that is, 'natural', man.

Failure to distinguish the ethical and nonethical dimension must result in the idea that the pure weak will and the impure but strong will are 'self-contradictory'. And it must result in the inability to distinguish, so to speak, between the ideas of the 'fanatic' and the 'angel'.

Now one might suppose that what distinguishes fanatical willing from the pure will is that the fanatic, unlike the saint (as I have argued), wills what he wills for his own sake. For does not he claim that his 'salvation' lies in his own greatness, or in the greatness of his cause? But this latter alternative shows we cannot make the distinction in the way suggested.

What is at the centre is, rather, the very concept of 'greatness'. For this concept has, in Kierkegaard's eyes, *no* intrinsic connection whatever with the concept of ethical goodness. That is not to say that it is not connected with some nonethical concept of 'the good of man'. Perhaps, indeed, the concept of greatness stands in some kind of inverse relationship to the ethical!

There are three distinct views here, all of which Kierkegaard must be taken to be denying.

There is the view that what is *great* is good — even from the ethical point of view. (Not that in the last resort the latter characterization allows this view to remain self-consistent.) This might be called a morality of the 'genius', or of the great man, somewhat in the spirit of Thrasymachus's or Nietzsche's ethical views. But it is certainly not the ordinary morality, and still less Kierkegaard!

There is the view that the so-called concept of the ethical good, that is, the concept of a species of the good occupying a categorically autonomous realm, is in fact confused — a pseudo concept. And for this confused pseudo concept we should substitute as the object of our admiration and our striving that genuine concept which is all that underlies the concept of goodness, namely, the concept of greatness. (This too represents, I think, a possible interpretation of Nietzsche's opinions.) Perhaps, one might call this a species of ethical naturalism.

There is, finally, the view that no such concept as 'ethically good', applicable to human beings, can make sense. The concept 'good', as a predicate of the human subject, actually means great.

Kierkegaard is, then, claiming that what is great is by no means necessarily good, from an ethical point of view, and that aiming at greatness is by no means a necessary or a sufficient criterion for the 'ethical will'; and that the concept of goodness is a concept that has a coherent ethical sense and represents the proper object of (is a criterion for) the ethical will. He is also claiming that greatness, of the object or of one's self (one's own will) is not a proper object of any ethical attitude, for instance, admiration or striving.

In sum, then, Kierkegaard claims that the fanatical and enthusiastic wills, and the ethical ideologies of fanaticism and enthusiasm, rely on construing concepts such as 'great', 'important', 'strong', 'exceptional', and 'impressive' as ethical concepts. (Most of these examples come from the relevant passage of Kierkegaard.) And that means: in Kierkegaard's view they are conceptually not relevant to questions of ethics. So the ethics of fanaticism or enthusiasm, the ethics of strength or greatness, rests on a simple failure to mark out the proper realm of the ethical.

(This category-claim, in Kierkegaard, like the similar claim in Kant, can, of course, be rejected either as false or as senseless. We are not logically bound by Kierkegaard's own ethical perceptions, including his perceptions of what the ethical amounts to. But if we reject his claims we must be prepared to reject the validity of the arguments he uses to support them, or the truth of the premisses on which those arguments rest. And to do this is, as far as I can see, to do no less than to suggest different criteria for the ethical: to express a fundamentally different perception of what the concept of 'the ethical' connotes. This is a difficult question, and I am not prepared to consider it here. But at least I should point out that it may not be, as people sometimes think, simply a matter of counterposing 'alternative' views of the ethical. For Kierkegaard, again like Kant, propounds arguments in favour of his categorization of the ethical. And it is arguable — and I would myself argue — that these arguments are at least extremely powerful, and very probably successful. In other words, I think it can be argued, as Kierkegaard argues, that the *rejection* of his criteria for the ethical is not in fact possible; and that the attempt *both* to reject his categorization of the realm of morality, *and* still to hold onto the idea that 'morality' is a conceptually autonomous realm, will be found to be self-contradictory. Thus, to reject his categorization is, implicitly or explicitly, to commit oneself to the denial of the autonomy of morality; and therefore to commit oneself to some form of 'naturalistic ethics', if not to some form of antimoralism.)

However, it is not a simple mistake to connect the notions of greatness and, more especially, strength, with morality. The ethics of fanaticism rests on a confused perception — a displacement — of a feature of morality that Kierkegaard regards as of the very first importance. This is expressed in the claim, 'All depends upon the will' (p. 62).

'All depends upon the will', a claim which Kierkegaard agrees with, can be taken in two ways. It may be taken to mean, and on this first interpretation it is false for Kierkegaard, that a man's human greatness rests in his 'fanatically' willing one thing, that is, in the strength and resoluteness of his will. Or it may be taken to mean, and then it is true, that salvation resides in the purity of the will: and that amounts to willing the Good.

Moreover, it is also true that the demand to will one thing is 'sublime' and 'severe' and uncompromising. And this point is emphasized by Kierkegaard, especially in his later, acknowledged writings. (Compare, on a nonreligious plane, Kant's characterization of the ethical demand as 'categorical'.) Here we might remember that the concept of total and absolute commitment is central in the argument of *Purity of Heart*.

This might be put in other terms. We might say: in considering the nature and content of the ethical (religious) demand, there can be no compromise with, no consideration for, ordinary human weakness of the will. That we are all in fact weak does not, in Kierkegaard's eyes, release us from the unconditional demands of morality, the unconditional will of God. It does not, as some might argue, imply that for mere human beings there must be a lower, less sublime, less severe, moral demand.

Now it is easy to confuse this claim with the quite different opinion that what is morally demanded of us is strength of will. But Kierkegaard does not hold this opinion, and in fact believes that it issues from an extremely grave misunderstanding of the whole nature of the ethical (the religious). For, in a word, to believe that among the ethical demands it is demanded that human beings be strong-willed, and to construe this belief not as a fanatic's morality, but rather as an approximation to the genuine ethicoreligious point of view indicated, is to fall into the generic error of 'Pelagianism'. (Otherwise, to repeat myself, it is to retreat into 'paganism'.) We cannot avoid noticing that Kierkegaard emphasizes here, as throughout his work, the absolute reliance of man upon the divine grace. He is, very roughly, an Augustinian.

He writes in the same passage, 'There is a power that binds him. He cannot tear himself loose from it. Nay, he cannot even wholly will it. For this power, too, is denied him' (p. 64). He is here speaking of the man who is, so to speak, defying the Good. And he identifies him with the fanatic, the man who places his entire ethical trust in his own strength of will. So the claim is *a*, that even such a man cannot get away from 'the Good' and hence his inevitable despair, while *b*, neither he nor anyone else can, of his own will alone, 'wholly will' the Good. And to supplement the partiality of man's willing of the Good, it is clear that 'grace', in the traditional terminology, is required.

It is therefore implied in the above passage, what Kierkegaard has elsewhere admitted, that even what approximates on earth, in the life of human beings, to 'purity of heart' is not and cannot of itself be a whole 'willing one thing in truth'. That no human being can, of himself and unaided by the Good, so to speak, genuinely will the Good in truth, or will one thing in truth.

I have so far talked almost entirely about the negative side of his ethical views, that is, the categorical distinctions by means of which he fences off his own (Augustinian) ethics from the various misinterpretations, all leading in the familiar way to some variety of subjectivism, with which Kierkegaardian ethics is apt to be confounded. I now want to fill out some of the positive apparatus, mostly implicit in *Purity of Heart*, though expounded explicitly in such later works as *Works of Love*, *Christian Discourses*, and *For Self-Examination*. Here, too, I shall be implicitly arguing that Kierkegaard's ethics, if examined, turns out to fall within a familiar Augustinian position.

There are three concepts which may be used to give content or body to the so far fairly abstract notion of 'purity of heart'. They are the concepts of *humility*, *self-sacrifice*, and *love (agape)*. Of these only the latter two are dwelt upon explicitly by Kierkegaard, but the former is very clearly implied in his attack upon the ethics of greatness and strength of will.

Kierkegaard has, so far, drawn a number of distinctions concerning the will, its modes, and its objects. He has distinguished the 'hardhearted' will from the loving will. And this amounts to a distinction between a will whose object is, or includes, the (ethicoreligious) good and happiness of all human beings, and one whose object (single, by hypothesis) excludes at least part of this. And this, in turn, amounts (I think) to the distinction between agape and all other frames of mind. For Kierkegaard certainly wants to define agape as a form of the will, rather than a form of the emotions or the intellect. Now agape, the loving will, can be conceived as an essential unity only on condition that its object be so conceived. And this means that the idea of the good and happiness of all human beings — of the human race, taken as a collection of individualism, not as world-historical entity — must be shown to be an essential unity. This is God. But all these proofs are still awaiting us.

He has distinguished willing the Good from willing the great, that is, drawn a conceptual distinction between two 'objects' of the will. This distinction of objects must, I argued earlier, be reflected in a distinction between the possible manners or 'modes' of willing the Good and willing the great. What the mode appropriate to willing the great is Kierkegaard hardly says: 'brazen, unholy enthusiasm' (p. 61) is not much help to us. But we may, I think, relate to willing the great the ideas of willing the impressive, willing the important, willing the exceptional, and willing the strong. So we are likely to think of such qualities as being impressed by, being overawed by, being overpowered by, being amazed by, and being interested or excited by something or someone. These, I suggest, are modes of the will which at least fall very close to those modes which reflect the object 'greatness'.

And certainly they all fall within what Kierkegaard called the realm of the aesthetic. He writes in his *Journals* (1852): 'I cannot possibly make it clear enough that the Exceptional has nothing whatsoever to do with ethics; ethically there is nothing exceptional, for the highest is quite simply what is demanded' (*Journals of Kierkegaard*, p. 477).

He has also distinguished the modes of strength of will (and its opposite, weakness of will) and purity of heart (and its putative opposite, sinfulness). Incidentally, it seems to follow from Kierkegaard's making and use of such a distinction that he cannot follow Kant's explanation of 'radical evil', and this despite the fact that he implies in the *Journals* that this theory is basically right (*Journals*, p. 193).

The latter distinction draws on a much more general category-distinction, namely, that between the nonethical ('aesthetic') categories and the ethical (ethicoreligious). Another example of this general distinction is the distinction between the ethical claim that purity is a good and the nonethical claim (to Kierkegaard, at least) that strength of will is a good; and similarly for their opposites.

That the pure will can be a loving will — given certain conditions concerning its object — has been argued. And this implies that its 'object' must be the true (ethicoreligious, that is, 'eternal') good of all men.

That the pure will cannot be either 'proud' or selfish' has been at least strongly suggested in Kierkegaard's attack on that confusion according to which 'purity' of the will is mistakenly construed as strength or enthusiasm. For the man who regards the strength of his willing as its (his) ultimate and only good is subject to what Christianity calls pride. (And this is the sin that lies at the root of the Pelagian error, according to orthodoxy.) And conversely, the man for whom strength and weakness are not *the* human good or evil, and who believes that the demand is for purity while purity, in human beings, is always necessarily flawed by our natural 'weakness', will see the demand for purity as involving a demand also for *humility*. For the demand for purity, allied with the recognition that purity can never be completely achieved because of his weakness, amounts to the recognition that man is necessarily subject to a condition (namely, his weakness) that stands in the way of his achieving what is categorically demanded of him. And this is humility.

The argument that the single-minded will is necessarily not self-centred is largely let go by default, since the most important of the opponents of Kierkegaardian 'objectivism' — those who support an ethics of pure fanaticism — agree with him that a criterion for the ethical is total commitment to something outside oneself, something that involves the ready possibility of self-sacrifice. Moreover, the idea of self-sacrifice seems to be implied in the idea of a love already mentioned. So to show that the genuine ethical will must be a form of love seems already to show that it must necessarily involve the possibility of self-sacrifice, that is, that it must be an essentially unself-centred, and unselfish, will.

Granted that the ethical will must involve love, humility, and self-sacrifice and must aim at the (ethical) good and happiness of all men, it does not follow that this concept of an ethical will has any real content. For that to be so it must be possible that someone's will should express love, humility, and self-sacrifice.

But what sort of proof is available for this kind of possibility? We are inclined to say, and as a first step rightly so, that only the exhibition of some actual individual whose will expresses these qualities will suffice. But this is not, of course, a mere matter of 'empirical' fact. For that he exhibits love, humility, and self-sacrifice cannot be at all a matter of empirical fact. For these are ethical characteristics. And that means, among other things, that they are characteristics of that individual regarded as an ethical subject, that is, as the possessor of an 'ethical will' (in the sense of a will capable of willing the ethically Good).

But that it is something of this kind that confronts one is clearly not a matter of fact. The ability to perceive the presence of ethical characteristics demands their presence in the perceiver. Thus the kind of 'proof' indicated for the possibility of the genuinely ethical will is itself one which can make sense (let alone appear valid) only for someone who is already himself in part at least committed to genuine ethical aims and demands.

The same, of course, is true for the distinctions drawn by Kierkegaard between ethical and nonethical concepts; for example, the claim that there is a genuine ethical concept of 'purity of heart' that is to be sharply distinguished from any nonethical concept, such as 'strength of will'. And here I repeat an admission made earlier.

Now Kierkegaard does in fact believe that there is, or 'was', such a man, a man whose will perfectly exhibited those three ethical characteristics, each sharply distinct from, and in some cases contrasted with, certain typically 'subjectivist' modes of the will, which guarantee at least the possibility of an ethical will. That man was Christ, the God-man.

It is therefore true, and must be immediately and fully admitted, that his 'proof' for ethics rests, among other premisses, upon *faith*, that is, upon the Christian faith in Christ the God-man.

And it is no use trying to construct a positive proof, starting, for example, from premisses of history and philosophy, that Christ was both man and God. For this would completely falsify a central element in Kierkegaard's theology: his insistent claim that the concept of the God-man is, for natural (commonsense and philosophical) reason a *paradox* and an offence, and something that is the proper object of *faith*, where 'faith' is distinguished as sharply as possible from any kind or degree of knowledge.

It is suggested, then, that it is possible for human beings to have faith in Christ, the God-man. And part of this faith is the belief that Christ's will and life perfectly exhibited those features of universal particularized love, humility, and self-sacrifice, that characterize the genuinely ethical will, the 'will for the Good'.

And this in turn guarantees the possibility of there being such a thing as the ethical will, so defined.

Notice how essential to this 'proof' is the claim that Christ was both God and perfect man. For, were his manhood (humility) not perfect, he could not stand as the pattern for our human wills to imitate. And were he not also divine, his will could not have exhibited in their full perfection those ethical qualities after which we must vainly strive.

In order to conclude the argument, we have to show that those nonethical modes of the will with which 'subjectivists' are apt to confound the Kierkegaardian ethics do not in fact allow the will to be described as genuinely 'essentially unified', that is, that they cannot in fact be species of 'willing one thing in truth'. And this is a demonstration that non-Kierkegaardian subjectivist autonomism is in fact incoherent, at any rate if construed (as is normal and natural) on a fundamentally Kantian or post-Kantian basis. And we have to show that those ethical modes of the will already indicated do in fact guarantee that the will is, in Kierkegaard's sense, single-minded in truth, and that such a will and its proper object are in fact essential unities.

Now Kierkegaard does suggest that the idea of 'willing one thing in truth' can be partly understood through two worldly approximations: two cases 'where there is some truth in the fact that he wills one thing' (p. 67). These are faithful love and devotion to a 'cause'. 'Some truth in' implies 'not the whole truth' or 'not complete truth in'. So Kierkegaard implies that neither faithful love nor devotion to a worldly cause can with complete truth be described as examples of 'willing one thing'. Each is an example, perhaps, of what we might call 'willing one thing in partial truth'.

Now it is easy to see why neither can involve 'complete truth'. For the objects of faithful love and devotion to a cause are human persons and human causes, for example, political or moral ones. And these are worldly objects, and so are changeable and mutable. So a will fixed upon some one human being (faithful love) or some one human cause (enthusiasm, devotion) can itself possess no more and no different kind of unity than does its object. And that is the 'contingent' unity of all worldly things.

And it is easy to see why Kierkegaard might want to describe such attitudes as involving 'partial truth'. For certainly they are what would normally be called single-minded. They are our paradigms for single-mindedness. But this answer is not enough. There are plenty of other attitudes which seem to deserve, according to that criterion, to be called 'willing one thing in partial truth', for example, a mania for death and destruction, or a lust after drink or sex. But quite certainly Kierkegaard would not regard these, as he regards faithful love and genuine devotion to a cause, as 'ladders' towards the genuine willing of the Good.

Clearly what distinguishes love and enthusiasm is that they involve self-abnegation. That is to say, they each involve, in somewhat different ways, those three ethical characteristics of the good will: love, humility, and self-sacrifice. ('Faithful love' itself involves, in Kierkegaard's eye, a readiness for self-sacrifice for the loved one and thus a certain kind of humility. And enthusiasm, being necessarily a form of self-sacrifice, similarly involves 'humility', that is, self-abasement before the cause. And the very word 'devotion' signifies the way in which something like love characterizes the enthusiast.)

However there are other reasons in Kierkegaard why these attitudes cannot perfectly exhibit those cardinal ethical qualities. Human love (*eros*, or *philia*) is, he says elsewhere, always and necessarily a form of self-love, that is, selfishness and self-centredness. So it cannot go with a total self-sacrifice, self-abandonment. And, I think, it is an attitude compatible with a certain kind of 'pride', which is related to the former point. Moreover, if we remember the attack on 'exclusiveness', it is clear that even love is capable of a great deal of inhumanity and hardheartedness—towards people other than the loved one. It is too 'particular' an attitude to meet Kierkegaard's criteria.

The opposite, perhaps, is true of enthusiasm: here it is, it seems, the cause that predominates, and the idea of the individual that is sacrificed in comparison.

If no human individual or cause can be the proper object of a genuinely and totally ethical attitude, for example, a genuine and total self-sacrifice, then the object of such an attitude can only be something—some person-like or cause-like being—that belongs not to the realm of the world but to the realm of the ethical (the 'eternal').

So, as far as we human beings are concerned, genuine 'purity of heart' is possible only on the additional assumption that there can be such an object for the will.

But for us the God-man is such an object. And so that faith which guarantees the possibility of there existing a 'paradigm' of genuine purity of heart also guarantees the possibility of there being an object for our pure willing.

CHAPTER 7

Kierkegaard's concept of truthfulness

One particular problem of Kierkegaard is expressed in this quotation: 'There is a "how" which has this quality, that if *it* is truly given, then the "what" is also given; and . . . it is the "how" of faith. Here, quite certainly, we have inwardness at its maximum proving to be objectivity once again' (*Journals of Kierkegaard* [1849], pp. 177–78). But how can an ethics of 'truthfulness' (authenticity) also be an ethics of 'truth'? How can it be both 'objectivist' and 'subjectivist'?

Behind this objection is the idea: the 'truth' of a belief, its 'content', is something independent of the believer and his condition; conversely, the 'truthfulness' of the believer (the 'how') is independent of the truth-value of the belief. The truth-values of statements ascribing belief are independent of the truth-values of the statements of those beliefs. The criteria for sincere belief are independent of the criteria for the truth of what is so believed. But Kierkegaard is speaking of the concept of truth in relation to the concept of self-knowledge and to the concepts of ethical and religious knowledge or belief.

His idea that this manner of belief also gives with itself a content is not merely a bit of bad psychology. It is not a causal connection. For he also says, 'in the spiritual world the form is the reduplication of the content' (*Authority and Revelation*, p. 43). And he says, 'the place and the path are within a man, and just as the place is the blessed state of the striving soul, so the path is the striving soul's continual transformation' (*Purity of Heart*, p. 84).

He also says, 'An objective uncertainty held fast in an appropriation-process of the most passionate inwardness is the truth, the highest truth attainable for an existing individual. . . . The truth is precisely the venture which chooses an objective uncertainty with the passion of the infinite' (*Concluding Unscientific Postscript*, p. 182).

Let us consider the concept of self-knowledge and the presumably correlative concept of a truth about oneself. Now it is clear that there is something odd about this concept. It is tempting to say: there cannot be any 'truth' about oneself, since this would presuppose that the self is some kind of natural object to which this 'truth' corresponds. So it would be wrong to say that self-knowledge is knowledge of the truth about oneself. Or, if we do say this, we must be using an essentially different concept of truth from, say, the concept of truth involved in geology or geography.

Self-knowledge must involve truthfulness. It cannot go together with self-deceit. If I am self-deceived, I am deceiving myself about myself, about a certain respect of myself. That is to say, I am not being truthful with myself about myself.

Now self-deceit seems to involve the 'what' of a false belief. For being self-deceived is surely believing something about yourself that is not true. Here already the normal distinction between sincerity and truth seems to break down. For otherwise it would make sense to describe the self-deceiver as sincerely believing something false about himself. Now there are people we can describe in these terms, but not the self-deceiver.

Self-deceit is a kind of 'believing what is not true' which could not be 'truthful'. It is a kind of 'what' which is also a 'how'. Perhaps there is something else at work too. For the self-deceiver is essentially someone who believes what is not true about himself. This is part of his aim. One might say: the self-deceiver has a commitment to believing what is not true about himself.

Could a man have the attitude characteristic of the self-deceiver (the 'how'), but as a matter of fact be correct about himself? Could he be essentially self-deceitful, yet as a matter of fact have self-knowledge? So, at any rate, his having self-knowledge is accidental and runs counter to his whole attitude.

One might ask: is there a sort of truth about persons (a 'what') which is determined by their attitude to the concept of a truth about themselves? Well, there is at any rate one: is a man interested, concerned in the truth about himself or is he not? Does he care about self-knowledge or does he not? For the truth about him is at least his: *how* he goes about things. 'Socrates was concerned to inquire into his own nature'. That is presumably a truth about Socrates. But it is one which Socrates himself made true in virtue of the way he went about this question. 'Anna deceived herself' is presumably a truth about Anna Karenina. But what makes it true is just that Anna was concerned to evade the truth about herself.

Inquiring into one's own nature—being truthful in this sense—is partly what might be called an act of will. It is a man's responsibility and choice, whether to deceive himself, or to remain ignorant of himself, or to try to find out the truth about himself. This is perhaps why Kierkegaard says, 'The ethical individual knows himself, but this knowledge is not a mere contemplation . . . it is a reflection upon himself which is itself an action, and therefore I have deliberately preferred to use the expression "choose oneself" rather than know oneself' (*Either/Or*, vol. 2, p. 263).

Whatever the concept of self-knowledge amounts to, it is clear that it involves the ethical. For discovering the truth about oneself is not something which can be done only in the objective spirit. One has the further responsibility of doing something about the self one has discovered. Either to accept it or to try to change it. Now someone deeply impressed with the achievements and spirit of 'objectivism' might object to this account. And if 'objectivity' is all that matters, he will be right. Kierkegaard says, of this possibility, that if 'the objective tendency is the way and the truth; the ethical is, becoming an observer. That the individual must become an observer is the ethical answer to the problem of life—or else one is compelled to assume that there is no ethical question at all, and so far no ethical answer' (*Concluding Unscientific Postscript*, p. 119).

Truthfulness, in general, is obviously an ethical concept. For being truthful is not a quality you either possess or do not possess accidentally. It is partly an attribute of the will. It presupposes freedom. So it is something that characterizes, not just the subject as part of nature, but the ethical subject.

Another way of describing the essentially truthful man—the man who is concerned about the truth in and for itself—is to say that he has a 'will for truth'. And that is to say: for him the idea of the truth plays the part of an ethical ideal. You might say: for him the truth appears a something of absolute value. You might also say: the truthful man can be described as a man who has made an absolute commitment to truth.

Now obviously this last statement has two quite different senses. You might mean simply that he does not know what the truth is, but whatever it is he is resolved to discover it. But you might mean he knows what the truth is, and it is to that that he is resolved to remain faithful. And these look quite different. But, once again, the latter meaning makes sense only if you presuppose that there is such a thing as 'the truth' which can either be known or not, and so forth. Now Kierkegaard, as I said, defined that concept of truth in which we are interested as 'an objective uncertainty held fast in an appropriation-process of the most passionate inwardness'. This is the commitment to truth. It shows why the two apparently different senses of being committed to truth cannot be held apart. For where there is no possibility of objective certainty, there is nothing more than objective uncertainty to be had in the realm of the objective. So what can being committed to the truth mean here? Like the first man, the truthful man does not know what the truth is: like the second man, he is resolved to stick by the objectively uncertain belief he has.

Introducing the concept of 'commitment' is implicitly introducing certain other ethical concepts, for instance the concept of 'the good'. In Kierkegaard's thought, the idea that the 'how' of faith also gives the 'what' of the faith is parallel to the idea that there is a 'how' of the will which also gives a certain 'what', that there is a certain manner of willing which also gives a certain object. His idea is that 'willing one thing', the willing that characterizes the absolutely committed man, can only be willing the Good.

The idea that willing single-mindedly is necessarily willing the Good is actually just another way of expressing the idea that thinking truthfully, as we might put it, is necessarily believing the Truth. It is not just an analogy.

The idea that willing single-mindedly is necessarily willing the Good is subject to the same kinds of doubt and puzzlement as the idea about truthfulness and truth. For instance, we want to object: but cannot a man single-mindedly will something which does not happen to be The Good?

We might say: it is not possible that there could be a 'how' of willing which has this quality, that if it is truly given, then the 'what' is also given! That is, we want to uphold the logical independence of the object of the will from the will's content, or manner.

Here it might be to the point to remember Kant. Kant worked a Copernican revolution in ethics as much as in epistemology. In ethics the revolution took the following form. Whereas previously philosophers had tried to define the good will by reference to a previously defined Good, Kant saw that this definition rested on confusing the natural and moral goods. The concept of a natural good, he argued, could be defined prior to the concept of the good will. But the concept of the moral good could not. In fact, Kant's revolution was this: to define the morally good in terms of the good will, that is, the will that obeys the moral law.

Kierkegaard often reads as if he is asserting the autonomy of morality and the moral will in Kant's manner. And indeed he was denying the heteronomy of morality. This interpretation would make his doctrine of the will familiar. But it cannot be completely correct, if only because he himself objects to a central feature of the Kantian autonomy; namely, the idea that moral law is law that the free will gives itself (see *Journals* [1850], p. 181). For he was a Christian.

I think Kierkegaard might argue: just as only the Good can be truly willed, so only The Truth can be truly believed, that is, believed in truthfulness. If an apparent 'truth' is not *The* Truth, then it cannot be believed—single-mindedly and wholly and purely. It cannot be something to which a man can make the absolute commitment characteristic of the commitment to the truth.

We may well use the concept of faith here. The view would be this: just as only the Good can be the object of that kind of Willing which we call 'faith', so only The Truth can be the object of that kind of belief which we call 'faith'. Not only 'just as': the two conditions are identical.

Like Kant, Kierkegaard partly identified the ethical and religious attitudes by their internal reliance on the concept of something absolute, unconditional, and categorical. (His exposition of this view is more powerful and persuasive than Kant's.) This is partly captured by the concept of a total commitment.

Consider what it means to believe in God—or, we might ourselves add, to believe in the goodness of human nature. Believing in God is unlike believing that it is about to rain in many ways. One is this. You can believe that it is about to rain in many ways: you can be concerned about it or unconcerned; you can be doubtful or sure. But you can believe in God only in one way— with the passion of the infinite and with faith.

For what sort of activity serves as criterion for a man's really and truly believing in God? I suggest his willingness to do all and suffer all for this belief, or rather for God. And this is expressed in his doing or suffering all, for instance, in his going to the stake.

But 'going to the stake' is also the criterion for a certain manner of belief. So here, perhaps, are certain kinds of belief which are such that the criterion for a man's truly believing is also a criterion for his believing deeply and passionately. One might still object. All this shows is that, in effect, there is a certain 'what' of belief which brings with it the 'how'—not vice versa. And it is not yet proven that a man cannot go to the stake for things which are wrong, even wicked!

Now one can make some reply to this. Whatever the martyr says his ideals are—however vile they appear in his mouth—still there is a certain pattern of self-sacrificing life and death which can only show that his real faith is that God is love. And nothing else can show this. Whatever he says does not count in the face of the evidence of his life and death. He shows himself to be a saint, even though to take his words seriously would be to think him a devil.

Certain ways of life express, willy-nilly, a certain typical belief or faith. But it can also be said of the martyr that his way of life and death expresses a certain manner of belief; namely, the manner of belief we might call 'the absolute commitment'. He has done and suffered all for his belief. So such a life and death is the only adequate expression for that commitment which can be called both a 'how' and a 'what' of belief.

I have used the concept of 'faith' here both because Kierkegaard does—it is obviously relevant to his interpretation of these doctrines in a peculiarly Christian sense—and because it seems to fit. For it is neither a clear concept of 'belief' nor a clear concept of 'will', yet it seems to be closely related to both. Certain sorts of belief can be adequately expressed only in modes of activity, or even by a man's whole way of life and resulting death. And these we may properly call 'faith'. (The use of this concept does not imply anything religious.)

Another point is this. Even if such a way of life and death shows that the man's belief amounted to a faith, a total commitment, still there can be a number of different faiths expressed in this life. It might be, for instance, the Feuerbachian faith that *man* is love!

But certainly this 'how' of life and death determines a certain range of beliefs. And if the 'how' involves, as I suggested, self-sacrifice and martyrdom for the sake of the belief, then *ipso facto* it must be essentially connected with the content of the belief that its holders should be prepared to sacrifice themselves that it prevail. So the content of the belief, too, is somewhat determined by the 'how' of its martyr's life and death.

There is only a certain range of beliefs to which a man can be totally committed, and this range is further restricted by the demand that this commitment essentially involve the possibility of self-sacrifice by suffering all for the belief.

I think there are other necessary restrictions on the sort of belief, or faith, which is expressed by the self-sacrificing way of life and death. One is, perhaps, that the martyr has to be understood as placing what might be called an 'absolute value' on the object of his commitment—God, human love, freedom and justice, or whatever it is. For the concept of being absolutely committed to something and the concept of placing an absolute value on it are obviously closely related. So it follows immediately that only objects which are intelligible to us as objects of an 'absolute' valuation can be intelligible objects of such a faith. To see the man as a martyr for his belief, we have to be capable of seeing his belief as something for which a man can intelligibly be martyred. (This may go some way to drawing the sting from the familiar objection of the 'sincere Nazi'.)

Another, more speculative restriction, is this: the martyr's life and death must be seen as expressing something like a worship or adoration of the object of his faith. He must appear as someone who is striving to attain a peak—ethical or religious—represented for him by his ideal. It has to be seen by us as something analogous to an object of *love* for God.

For Kierkegaard that way of life and death which truly expresses a man's true will for the Good, and his true belief in the Truth, also expresses his true *love* for the truly lovable God.

Indeed both the commitment to the Good described as the single-minded willing and the commitment to the Truth described as inwardness or 'truthfulness' are forms of love: love of the Good and love of the Truth respectively. The 'truthful' man can naturally be described as the man who 'loves' truth. Kierkegaard deals with this concept on three levels: the aesthetic, the ethical, and the religious. We might say he points to three conceptions of love (see *Either/Or*, *Stages on Life's Way*, and *Works of Love*). The aesthetic concept of love is that captured in the ordinary idea of 'falling in love': love as a profound passion. The ethical concept of love, following Hegel, he identifies as expressed in the married life. The religious concept is expressed in the life of Christian charity: the works of love.

The way of life and death of the martyr is that which expresses Christian charity, *agape*. This way of life is also the expression for the absolute commitment characteristic of faith. This form of love is, then, seen as a manifestation of the will, which is why the Gospels tell us, 'Thou shalt love'. Of this I cannot speak here.

Marriage is that expression for love which most nearly approximates to the Christian life. And both the concepts of faith and commitment are closely related to the concept of marriage. We speak of a 'faithful' married life. What does this 'faith' amount to? Primarily a commitment, namely, a commitment to the other party. This is not to say any particular commitment. For what the commitment in question is depends in part on what the other party's desires and interests happen to be. One might say an absolute respect for the other is demanded, and that the other is seen, in a sense, as an absolute value, that is, as something which gives a sense to the whole of one's life. This is not a familiar feature of the concept of marriage, but a profoundly valuable one.

Marriage can be seen as an approximation to the life of the Christian. But in it one's spouse takes the place of God, or Christ. And this accounts for an incoherence in the very concept of marriage. For no human being can, still less should, take the kind of place in a person's life that a God can and maybe should take. A way of life which shows that the person who leads it has towards a *human being* the kind of attitude characteristic of the Christian religion also shows that he is what we might call idolatrous. For example, it may make sense within the religious framework to go to one's martyrdom for the sake of the faith, since to speak of the religious framework is to imply that this *death* is given sense in terms of the concepts of eternity, immortality, and salvation. But we could not give any such sense to a death whose framework was simply the ethical concept of marriage.

The point might be put more strongly, although it becomes dangerous. That attitude towards the ethical which expresses itself in talk of 'absolute values' and 'unconditional' or 'categorical' duties, and the like, cannot be made sense of unless understood as conceptual shorthand for an expression of a religious attitude towards life. For what sense can be made of the idea that a man's ethical duty is to do all and suffer all for the truth, the Good? What can give sense to a purely ethical martyrdom?

Still, the ethical concept of marriage is near enough to the religious concept of charity to have some sense. This is less true of the aesthetic notion of love. What sense could be made of the concepts of faithfulness and obligation in connection with this?

Marriage presupposes a commitment, but falling in love does not. Marriage is therefore a concept involving the concept of the free will, but love is not. For this reason the idea of a 'duty to love' can make no sense in the aesthetic categories. If there is no commitment of love, there cannot be those *grounds* for obligations and responsibilities that exist in the case of marriage or the Christian commitment. There can be nothing to give any *content* to any such obligations or responsibilities. Or rather, there can be only the will of the other party if, indeed, the other party is concerned!

Analogous to the view that there is a 'how' of belief which brings with it the 'what', namely, the Christian faith, we might construct a doctrine about love. Just as truthfulness, the 'how' of belief, brings with it The Truth, its 'what'; so 'true love' necessarily brings with it a certain object of love—the truly Lovable.

In the light of Kierkegaard's analysis of the facets of the concept of love, what sense could we make of the concept of 'true love'? Obviously, the way of life characteristic of Christian charity will be said to express true love. For neither the ethical life of marriage nor the aesthetic life—if there is one—of love can express fully and coherently anything like a willed commitment.

Obviously you can be in love with pretty well anybody, good or evil. And obviously you can be married to pretty well anybody.

But in the latter case your faithfulness does express at least that you see your spouse as, so to speak, a value. But, as I argued, incoherently.

The concept of a love which is expressed essentially in the commitment to do all and suffer all for the loved object is a concept which can be adequately and intelligibly embodied only in the way of life and death characteristic of Christian self-sacrifice. And this way of life and death also embodies the faith in God, who is the truly Lovable. So we could again say: the 'how' of love gives also a 'what'.

In his volume of Christian discourses called *Works of Love* Kierkegaard comments on Saint Paul's remark, 'Love believes all things'; he adds, 'and yet is never deceived' (p. 213). Now taken in the obvious sense this observation is absurd, perhaps self-contradictory. To believe all things—or anything—is surely just to lay yourself open to deceit! Surely to avoid being deceived the only sure thing is not to believe anything—to be totally sceptical. So Kierkegaard here contrasts the attitude characteristic of love with the attitude of mistrustfulness. Love involves trust, a kind of faith. For the man of love to believe is to have made a commitment to believe.

The point is this: truth and deception are always and necessarily the two equal possibilities. It is not that 'knowledge' decides whether truth or deception is present. For knowledge is itself only knowledge of possibilities. Then your choice between these two, truth or deception—whether you choose to believe or mistrust—shows which of the pair loving/mistrustful you are.

Kierkegaard is here speaking mainly of the knowledge that we may have of other people, the kind of knowledge about them that is usually thought necessary for any sort of ethical judgement to be well-grounded. It is essential to his position that this kind of knowledge can never be complete. This amounts to precisely the same as saying: it is impossible that a man could ever be faced consciously with the objective truth about another man.

There seem to be two reasons for this statement. First, that 'the only reality that exists for an existing individual is his own ethical reality' (*Concluding Unscientific Postscript*, p. 280) — not anybody else's. And this expresses a common enough view. Second, that although there may *be* the possibility of objective knowledge of others — up to a point — still, as ethical subjects, we are not concerned with this sort of knowledge. As ethical subjects we are concerned with other people 'ethically', so even if a man is faced with what amounts in fact to the objective truth about another man, still it is not *as* objective truth that it faces him. It does not, for example, present itself merely *as* a piece of information, or as part of a systematic theory of human nature. This man's attitude to this truth cannot be the attitude of an observer of human beings.

As an ethical subject he must be in some 'ethical position' relative to the other man. I do not mean just in some ethical role. I mean that he must be ethically concerned about the other man. And there seem to be two broad possibilities here. Either he must be ethically concerned in the way characterized by the broad concept of love, or in the way characterized by the concept of mistrustfulness. For between these lies only indifference; and that is the attitude characteristic of the objective, the observer.

As far as the mere observer is concerned, there can never be enough evidence in the man's ethical character. We are never, so to speak, scientifically warranted in issuing ethical judgements about others. So it is not the case that there is this third possibility besides the possibilities of love and mistrust. These amount to either believing in the man, ethically speaking, or not believing in him. That is, roughly, either believing he is ultimately good, or believing he is ultimately evil.

So Kierkegaard's position seems to be this: we cannot avoid taking up one of these two positions relative to other people. And to take up either position is to make a decision, a choice, which reveals, itself, what sort of person the chooser is.

The position, or attitude, characteristic of love and the position characteristic of mistrust are both what we might call 'ultimate commitments'. They are both answers to the question: what is human nature ultimately like, ethically considered? Are men fundamentally good or evil? Like any fundamental commitment, these will express themselves in certain broad patterns of life and death. These are so broad that it is not easy to say anything definite about them.

But this might be said about the commitment characteristic of love: the commitment of trust, one might call it. The way of life and death of the man whose commitment *this* is must be such as to exhibit his love, his trust, of others. The obvious example in literature is Dostoyevsky's Prince Myshkin, whom everyone calls an 'idiot'.

There is now a fairly obvious sense in which we might say that such a man cannot be deceived. For there cannot be anything in his life which is such as to prove to him that his view of men is mistaken. The Lisbon earthquake, like the German extermination camps, has no force whatever as a *proof* that optimism is an intellectual error. For, worse, optimism and the attitude of the man of Christian love are not *intellectual* positions at all. They are ethical commitments, and it does not make sense to talk of a commitment of *this* kind being proved mistaken by events. But, we might object, in this sense neither does it make sense to suppose that the fundamentally mistrustful man can be deceived!

But this is not Kierkegaard's view, oddly enough. His view seems to be this: the mistrustful man not only can be deceived, but always is deceived, for he always deceives himself. He deceives himself 'out of the highest', says Kierkegaard (*Works of Love*, p. 221). He adds: 'According to this view to be deceived signifies simply and solely to quit loving, to be carried away to the point of abandoning love in and for itself, and in this way to lose its intrinsic blessedness' (*Works of Love*, p. 223).

What way of life and death might embody this fundamental mistrustfulness, that is, this fundamental refusal to believe in people or to have faith in them? Well, certainly one that is the antithesis of the Christian way of life. It is pretty clear that a life of loving self-sacrifice must be the antithesis of *this* way of life.

The Christian way of life expresses not just a faith, a belief in the absoluteness of certain values, but also an attitude to human beings. For it is an essential part of that way of life that sacrifice is made of oneself for others, in such a way that one's sacrifice expresses what might be called an absolute love for them—or the nearest we can coherently come to love. It thus expresses a commitment, not just to some value or other, but also to the value of human beings as embodying this value. It expresses a commitment that characterizes the man of 'love'.

If one tries to think of a way of life whose antithesis this is, one may well picture the kind of life Hobbes ascribes to man in the state of nature. It will be essentially a life expressing a fundamental self-interest, a life in which self-interest can be seen to play the central and forming part. In fact, it is tempting to suppose that it can only be a way of life that is such as to express a fundamental absence of any central ethical commitment, and a way of life that expresses either a Thrasymachean denigration of the demands of morality or a Nietzschean dismissal of these demands.

Then we might well say that the fundamentally mistrustful man is necessarily deceived about one big thing: the importance and perhaps the existence of the moral demands. This is not, of course, to say that he will be deceived in matters of fact, in ordinary everyday mundane matters: indeed, probably not. But it might now be called a necessary truth that the mistrustful man is a man who cannot see the ethical for what it is. And this is certainly a serious blindness or error. There could be none more serious, ethically speaking. The form of deceit the mistrustful man is subject to is *self-deceit*. For nobody else is deceiving him. Or rather, nobody else can do for him what he has in effect done: made the commitment to mistrust and disbelief, the commitment away from trust and love.

One might call this the commitment away from the ethical point of view, if this description did not contain a contradiction.

For surely the way of life which expresses the fundamentally mistrustful point of view is not the kind of way of life which can be seen as expressing a 'commitment' of any kind. For it cannot be seen as expressing the commitment to any *value*. Except, say, the supposed 'value' of preserving oneself from being deceived, at all cost.

There is, after all, an asymmetry between the mistrustful and loving man. For the mistrustful man, it now appears, there can really *be* no such thing as an 'ethical truth'. It is hard to see how there can be an ethical *anything* for him—except, perhaps, himself and his own self-defined self-interests. But for the loving man there cannot help but be an ethical truth. We may put it thus. If the ethical is not just one vast illusion, then the mistrustful man is necessarily wrong and the loving man necessarily right. So the life of charity does at any rate express the truth that ethics is not an illusion. We could also say: there *is* an ethical reality.

If there is an ethical reality, then the human individual is really the ethical subject. So the life of charity may be seen as expressing that insight too. Thus, I think, it can be seen as expressing a form of general self-knowledge; namely, the knowledge that one is oneself an ethical subject and, in a way, *the* ethical subject. And this general self-knowledge is the basis for a certain form, or manner, of self-inquiry which in turn gives one the possibility of self-knowledge in its more usual sense.

For, insofar as self-knowledge is an ethical concept, the concept of something with an ethical content and ethical implications, it must of course presuppose the perception that one is oneself a being properly subject to this category of knowledge.

Thus the possibility of the attitude I earlier described as the commitment to truth (truthfulness) rests on possession of the attitude whose most adequate expression is the life of Christian charity.

Of the mistrustful man we shall have to say something like this. There are certain forms of self-knowledge, and knowledge of others, open to him. But there is one form of self-knowledge which is not. It is not open to him to pursue self-knowledge in the ethical spirit and so to acquire self-knowledge as an ethical subject. He cannot be, in that sense, truthful. He cannot be committed to the truth, in that sense.

The mistrustful man's sort of self-knowledge must be distinguished from the sort of self-knowledge available to the man whose point of view is just objective. The latter must have a picture of himself which is removed even further from anything ethical. There is no room in this picture for any ethical concept.

The mistrustful man, though, has in a sense an ethical, subjective, point of view. He has *attitudes* towards other people and presumably towards himself too. As I said earlier, he has that attitude we might describe as not believing in human nature. So for him there can be no *point* in ethics. If we like, we can still claim that he has a kind of ethical point of view—he is certainly not purely 'objective' in his attitudes to others—but only, it seems, by claiming that the egoism his life expresses is a kind of ethical attitude.

Since his mistrustfulness expresses the failure to value people, he must either give himself a special ethical position or place on himself the low ethical value he places on others. In the first case, he will necessarily be under the illusion, from the ethical point of view, of being a special case. In the second case, he will be debarred from seeing himself, just as he is debarred from seeing others, as an object worthy of that respect which characterizes the ethical point of view: the point of view expressed by the life of Christian charity. In either case he has cut himself off from a whole dimension of self-knowledge.

The asymmetry between the cases of the mistrustful and loving men can be described like this. For both it is intelligible to speak of an ethical 'truth'. Only the mistrustful man's concept of this 'truth' is necessarily limited or distorted in comparison with the man of charity's concept. Their concepts are enough similar to be comparable, and in this comparison the limited concept must be rejected. The mistrustful man will, of course, claim that the loving man is under an illusion about the nature of ethical reality. And the loving man will make the same claim about him.

But if the loving man is under an illusion, then, I think, an attempt to describe the world in his supposedly ethical terms must run into incoherence. For his illusion is precisely the extent to which ethical terms can be used in describing the world.

However, it does not seem that we can describe the life of the Christian saint only incoherently. That the description looks incoherent if construed from the nontheistic point of view is neither here nor there. Taken on its own terms it is perfectly coherent.

If I am right, it follows that the mistrustful man's claim that the saint is under an illusion about the nature of ethical reality is itself merely the expression of an illusion. He is under the illusion that, because *he* cannot make sense of the saint's way of life, neither can the saint.

But I do not think the similar claim about the mistrustful man's outlook, made by the saint, is similarly deluded. Thus, I believe, there is an inescapable asymmetry — one might even call it a 'logical' or 'conceptual' asymmetry — between these two ethical outlooks.

index